A CARTOON WAR

The Tiger: 'Curious! I seem to hear a child weeping!'

*Fierce antagonism to Germany in the First World War gave Clemenceau
his nickname, Tiger; Will Dyson's prophetic cartoon appeared
in the* Daily Herald *in 1919.*

Joseph Darracott

A CARTOON WAR

World War Two in Cartoons

LEO COOPER
LONDON

Dedication

To my friends at the Imperial War Museum both now and when I worked there.

My sincere thanks to Anne Channon, Gordon Daniels, John Dower, Penelope Driver, Meirion Harries, Michael Nicholson, Liz Ottaway, Alex Potts and Peter Simpkins for a medley of advice, translation, support and criticism. My gratitude to the Imperial War Museum's Departments of Art, Photographs and Printed Books for facilities. My added thanks to my family and other helpful friend. However, I take responsibility for any faults found in this book; I shall be glad to hear from readers who can correct or better inform me.

First published 1989 by Leo Cooper

Leo Cooper is an independent imprint of the Octopus Publishing Group, Michelin House, 81 Fulham Road, London SW3 6RB

LONDON   MELBOURNE   AUCKLAND

Copyright © 1989 Joseph Darracott

This book conceived, edited and designed by E.T. Archive, P.O. Box 190, London SW7 1NW

Designed by Karen Osborne
Edited by Tom Hartman
Picture research by Joseph Darracott and Anne-Marie Ehrlich

ISBN: 0-85052-1653

Acknowledgements

Every effort has been made to trace the copyright owners of the illustrations. Any ommissions will be corrected in a subsequent printing if the publishers are informed.

Associated Newspapers, p.70, 77, 94.
The Bulletin, p.15.
Cartoon Study Centre, University of Kent at Canterbury, p.67, 70, 77, 78.
Chicago Daily Tribune, p.128.
© DACS 1989, p.119, 122, 124, 125.
Daily Mirror, p.57, 83, 89, 96 top.
Courtesy of John Dower, p.53, 61, 63 left, 137, 138, 139.
Imperial War Museum, p.18, 24 left, 80, 81.
Inter-Continental Features/L'il Abner Estate, p.20; /McNaught Syndicate, p.51, 55; /Milton Caniff, p.56.
King Features Inc, p.13, 91-3, 123 right.
London Express News and Features, p.66, 78, 85, 153.
Melbourne Argus, p.132.
John Murray Ltd, p.72, 127.
N.E.A. Service, USA, p.34.
© 1942, 1970, *The New Yorker Magazine, Inc*, p.73, 75, 130, 145.
Sir Gordon Minhinnick/*New Zealand Herald*, p.62, 131.
Punch, p.9, 36, 97, 99, 115, 141, 147.
St Louis-Post Dispatch, p.38, 52.
School of Slavonic Studies, p.16, 111, 114.
Ronald Searle, p.146.
Mrs E. Sherriffs, p.17.
Solo Syndication, p.16 right, 30,37, 67, 100, 104, 105, 110, 117, 140, 144, 152.
Saul Steinberg, p.21.
The Sun p.12.
Wiener Library, p.52, 103.

Printed and bound in Great Britain by
Redwood Press Limited, Melksham, Wiltshire

Contents

Chapter 1

WAR LEADERS AND SYMBOLS

The story begins with lunch in a London restaurant some years before the war. The party consisted of Bernard Partridge and Leonard Raven Hill, both from *Punch*, and a younger cartoonist from the *Evening Standard*, David Low. Partridge and Low had decided to meet because on one occasion the same idea had occurred to both of them, and they had drawn almost the same cartoon. Low found his companions ultra-conservative, even reactionary, but he enjoyed the shop talk very much, especially discussing symbols.

The *British Lion*, we all three agreed, certainly had his points as a cartoon 'property'. With his waving mane and his tufted tail he could be made to look very striking, crouching in dignified anger or glaring nobly at nothing. He made what they called 'powerful' cartoons. But apart from this purely aesthetic consideration, there seemed no justification for continuing to libel the British people by likening it to this unworthy creature, notoriously a loud roarer but a cruel and cowardly beast, only bold when facing something weaker than itself.

The *Punch* cartoonists did not accept Low's strictures, however, on nations and ideas represented by women. Low argued:

HITLER

The Russian team of cartoonists known as Kukryniksy show Goebbels painting an adulatory portrait of Hitler. Goebbels boasted that the creation of the Hitler legend was one of the most important things he had done for the National Socialist party.

THE UNHOLY ALLIANCE
'A sword in front, and a dagger behind.'

The allies are Roosevelt, Churchill, Stalin, Chiang Kai-shek, Giraud, Beneš, de Gaulle, Mihailovič, and Tito.

The personification of the higher abstractions as beautiful females was a convention handed down from our unsophisticated forefathers. To put it mildly, they overdid it. To them *Justice*, recognized in these later times as a stern cold unfeminine virtue (unlike *Mercy*, *Hope*, *Love*, etc.), was rather absurdly a woman; as also was *Liberty*: the most virile of human ambitions; and *Peace*, the business of strong men, still impersonated by that futile maiden carrying the allegedly peaceful but actually rather quarrelsome bird, the dove.

Low was keen to find new symbols, and to avoid those which were worn out or misleading (among his own innovations was a double-headed mule for the Lloyd George and Bonar Law coalition government). His companions vigorously defended using existing symbols and

signs that their public understood. Low remembered the lunch as 'one of the genuinely delightful spots' of his life. 'We disagreed frequently and emphatically, we each consumed two helpings of roast duck and we parted friends.'

Such a conversation could have taken place in many different places at that time. There was a widely felt need for a language of cartooning which would be understandable and effective. Perhaps David Low was over-anxious about fading symbols. They continued to suit *Punch* well enough for some years still, and certainly through the Second World War. But Low's own problem of communicating with readers was rather more insistent than that of his *Punch* colleagues, since he worked for a daily paper while they worked for a weekly. He had the

München, 28. April 1940
45. Jahrgang / Nummer 17

30 Pfennig

SIMPLICISSIMUS
VERLAG KNORR & HIRTH KOMMANDITGESELLSCHAFT, MÜNCHEN

Verzweiflung in London · Disperazione a Londra

„Zerbrichst du deinen Regenschirm, zerknicke ich meine Zigarre!"
"Se tu spezzi l'ombrello, io stritolo il sigaro!„

DESPAIR IN LONDON
'You break your umbrella. I'll destroy my cigar.'

*Olaf Gulbransson, as remarkable for his powers of
characterization as his finely tuned sense of design, has
used tabs of identity for this cartoon of Chamberlain and
Churchill. A mainstay of* Simplicissimus, *Gulbransson had
many imitators and tremendous popularity. He returned to
his native Norway in the 1920s, but then took up residence
again in Germany, where he continued to draw for*
Simplicissimus *until it ceased publication in 1944.*

more urgent need to be up to the minute, and to
highlight the news as it arose. It was also part of
his stock in trade to enjoy provoking controversy.
As a fellow cartoonist wrote in 1938, 'Low is a
political rowdy, and as such, a most amusing
nuisance.'

By the end of the 1930s there was a
worldwide audience for newspaper cartoons,
both on international and domestic events. Low
was lucky in having the freedom to choose his
subjects and their treatment written into his
contract. 'Policy': it read, 'It is agreed that you
are to have complete freedom in the selection
and treatment of subject matter for your
cartoons and in the expression therein of the
policies in which you believe.' Other cartoonists
saw their jobs differently; Norman Lindsay in
Australia took the view that as a cartoonist,
policy was not his concern. In other countries
restrictions were placed on comment not only
by editors but also by the state.

Battles for the freedom of the press had been
fought fiercely in the nineteenth century. Cartoons and caricature were valuable political
weapons, encouraged when supportive and
liable to be suppressed when hostile to a
government in power. The First World War had
seen much cartooning in the service of national
causes, an activity which some cartoonists
combined with poster design. Newspaper and
magazine cartoonists continued to work as
poster artists in the Second World War, notably
in Russia. Indeed, the dividing line between the
different uses of drawings, whether for political
comment or propaganda, is a shaky one.

No national press is free in time of war,
though the character and degree of government
control varies greatly. The Second World War

was no exception. Cartoonists did not have a choice about whether to follow national policies if their work was to be printed. Indeed, one role for cartoonists was to act like government spokesmen. There was no doubt that the Minister of Propaganda in Germany was a puppet master; in other countries the relations between government and the press were less clear-cut. Indeed, one civil servant in the equivalent British Ministry of Information described it in the first years of the war as 'a perfectly useless body'. David Low pointed up the contrast between German and British organizations with a cartoon on the worst story and the best propaganda (Germany) and the best story and the worst propaganda (Britain).

Issues about the freedom of the press mainly concern editorial cartoons, appearing in newspapers or political magazines; it is here that politicians and war leaders are depicted, and international events receive comment. The use of the word 'cartoon' to describe such drawings goes back to *Punch* in 1843, when John Leech drew a series of graphic satires of competition designs (correctly called 'cartoons', as are also drawings on paper for tapestries) for pompous frescoes proposed for the walls of the Houses of Parliament. *Punch* had a clear right to use the term, since for more than a hundred years two drawings appeared each week commenting on events. Newspapers also employed editorial cartoonists, who had the difficult job of responding daily to news. Terms in different countries do not altogether correspond to the usage in English, where the tendency is to extend 'cartoon' to a term embracing editorial cartooning, strip cartoons, comic books, animated film and portrait caricature, as well as visual gags.

THE DOCTOR'S DILEMMA
Hitler: 'Sorry I can't do more – I'm feeling a bit shaky myself. I've just had an accident with a bear.'

This cartoon by Bernard Partridge appeared in Punch *in June, 1943, after Mussolini had survived an assassination attempt; Hitler's military reverses in Russia make the comparison. Partridge's career on the* Punch *staff began in 1891 and he became the principal cartoonist in 1909. His fine academic draughtsmanship uses extensive hatching, which had been a feature of* Punch's *nineteenth-century black and white drawings.*

In German *Karikatur* is a generic term; in French, cartoonists are often known as *humoristes*; strip cartoons have a separate designation in French as *Bandes Dessinées*, while in Italian *Fumetti* describes a variety of cartooning, including strip cartoons.

This digression into European or other languages could be extended, but it is enough to say here that the editorial cartoon is the centre of the selection of images in this book. They are the most explicit commentaries on history as it happens, and to make their messages clear they employ a special range of techniques.

Many editorial cartoons in the war focused on national leaders. These men are the key members of a cast of characters acting on the world stage. Chubby-faced Churchill, toothbrush-moustached Hitler, fat Göring, Stalin with a

'To the fortifying of Italo-Albanian friendship.'

The ingenuity of this cartoon by Kukryniksy rests in superimposing animals on the European map, making Italy about to devour Albania. It is the situation seen from Russia in 1939. The collective name Kukryniksy came from the first letters of the artists' names: Mikhail Vasilievich KUprianov, Porfiry Mikitovich KRYlov, and NIKikolai Alexandrovich Sokolov.

drooping moustache – all these were instantly recognizable. They each had what David Low called 'tabs of identity'. The faces of other important people, such as military and naval commanders, were far less well-known; when they appear in editorial cartoons, they frequently have names written on them for identification.

The figure identified by a tab does not necessarily have much to do with what the person depicted actually looked like. Some sitters were notoriously difficult to portray. The editorial cartoonist's task is to find a formula into which to fit the public personality, whom the cartoonist may then place in a good or poor light. Churchill may be taken as an example. Low had this to say: 'He belongs to that sandy type which cannot be rendered properly in black and white. His eyes, blue, bulbous and heavy-lidded, would be impossible.' Churchill in British cartoons soon acquired a folder of tabs of identity – his cigar, the V for Victory sign which he popularized, a liking for wearing different hats, his practical zipped overalls nicknamed a siren suit, while his hobby of bricklaying became as well-known as Gladstone's enjoyment in cutting down trees. In enemy cartoons Churchill's appearance turns from benevolence to aggressive cruelty, his cigar becomes a symbol of greed, and his round face seems the evident result of self-indulgence.

Major leaders, once identified, can speak the lines a cartoonist writes for them. Dialogue is the common form for an editorial cartoon, since more than three people in conversation makes it very difficult to get a point across. The leaders may be speaking as themselves, or on behalf of their countries, as substitutes for those national symbols which *Punch* in its old-fashioned way

'Let us mercilessly smash and destroy the enemy.'

This poster image of a Russian soldier bayoneting Hitler is a characteristically violent image against a leader consistently ridiculed by the artists. Hitler's head appears through the text of the Russo-German Pact, his mask of friendship fallen away.

'It's all Greek to me.'

George Whitelaw's cartoon appeared in the Daily Herald, *commenting on Mussolini's lack of success in the Greek war. A laurel wreath is a classical reminder of Mussolini's imperial ambitions.*

continued to employ. National symbols had declined in importance since the First World War, partly because the person of the Kaiser Wilhelm II was used by anti-German cartoonists as a symbol of militarism and evil. Louis Raemaekers and Will Dyson produced horrifying Kaiser images, far surpassing in vicious cruelty the previous bogeymen cartooned, like Bismarck or Napoleon. The very extreme caricature of the Kaiser incidentally made it more possible to distinguish between the leaders and the led, militarists and ordinary Germans. This again became a relevant issue in the Second World War when those in propaganda ministries puzzled over whether to blacken entirely the name of the enemy or seek to divide enemy opinion; and on a more significant scale the issue arose on the question of whether to insist on unconditional surrender for Italy, Germany and Japan.

There is no nuance in symbolizing a country by an animal. The main symbols in Europe are of long standing, and derive originally from heraldry. This is true of the British lion, for example, and the Austrian and German eagles, as well as the American eagle. The Russian bear is an exception. Other countries at war had no such easily identifiable symbols, though characteristic animals and birds were adopted for countries like Australia (the kangaroo), Canada (the beaver), South Africa (the springbok), and New Zealand (the kiwi). In the East more abstract symbolism is the rule (the Japanese Imperial crest is a stylized chrysanthemum), which means that colours such as white for purification of the spirit, or the cleansing rays of the sun, need decoding in Japanese cartoons. In enemy cartoons of Japan, the readily recog-

'He's right, Joe. When we ain't fighting we should act like sojers.'

Mauldin tells a good story about this cartoon. An inexperienced colonel arrived in North Africa who missed the irony of this rather subversive comment, and seriously thought of reproducing it widely to encourage higher standards of dress and deportment; but he dropped the idea, to Mauldin's relief.

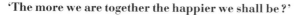

'The more we are together the happier we shall be?'

Well, not quite, since the sarcastic implication of this cartoon by Carlos is that Churchill and Roosevelt are foolish to rely on Stalin's good will. The long and distinguished career of Carlos in Argentina began in the early years of the century; and by 1935 he was the regular cartoonist of Careta, *which he continued to be until his death in 1950. His work included comic strips and children's book illustration.*

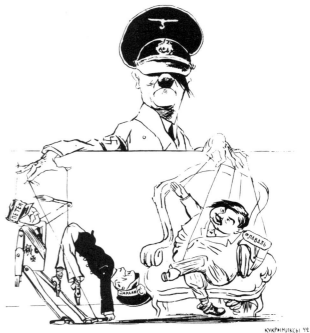

THE PUPPET MASTER

Hitler is seen by Kukryniksy as the manipulator of the French leadership, Pétain, Laval and Darlan. The picture is of a kind which editorial cartoonists often aim at, showing secret truth behind appearances.

'He can take it.'

nizable figure of a Samurai warrior is frequent.

Fables and animal stories are common currency in cartoons, whether from East or West. Every paper could expect references to folk tales and children's stories to be understood, whether Momotaro (the Peach boy) in Japan, or Jack and the beanstalk in the West. Some literary papers were more demanding. Bernard Partridge came from an older generation for whom classical references and quotations from Shakespeare came easily. The pages of *Punch* therefore contain not only the nations personified by human figures like John Bull, Uncle Sam or Marianne, but also classical gods and goddesses; and situations are taken from history and drama. Classical allusions were a favourite way of putting Mussolini in his place; on some occasions Julius Caesar seemed more useful, while Hitler found himself in the harsh spotlight of Macbeth.

ПОПУРРИ ИЗ УКРАИНСКИХ ПЕСЕН, ЗАПИСАННЫХ НА ХАРЬКОВЩИНЕ
И ПОЛТАВЩИНЕ.

'Gad, sir. Lord Dolt is right. We must open hostilities against Russia or there is a grave danger that Hitler will lose the war.'

Krokodil, *like other satirical papers everywhere, made use of its title as a personality who could appear on the cover or in other parts of the paper including the cartoons. The musical crocodile is in a good humour on this occasion.* Mr Punch *was apt to make more solemn appearances; he might congratulate a victor, but he also rebuked politicians if he thought fit.* Punch's *policy line for cartoons was decided by a convivial weekly meeting at the* Punch *table.*

David Low's most famous character was often found, as here, steaming in a Turkish bath, and pontificating to a friend, sometimes the cartoonist himself. Low intended Blimp to exemplify muddle-headedness – many of his statements contain inner contradictions; but Blimp escaped from his creator to become a military and political fogey. Blimp's name was borrowed for a film which ran into trouble with censorship. He was even borrowed in Russia by Efimov to complain about the slowness of Britain in opening a Second Front. Low angrily drew a Russian Blimpski which Russian publications declined to print.

The main humorous journal in Russia, *Krokodil*, took a far more direct and aggressive line. *Punch* stood for stability and the endurance of British traditional values, but the tone of *Krokodil* was strident and polemical. The stock figures of Russian caricature were rarely from a past which the revolution had repudiated and, instead, symbolized the present. The virtuous citizen, the valiant soldier, the persistent industrial worker — all of these are pitted against unjust owners of capital, greedy exploiters of labour, and the ideological enemies of socialism. The period following the Russo-German Pact was a difficult time, but, once Germany had invaded Russia, the force of polemical imagery could be released. The German enemy, and particularly the leaders, were thrustingly vilified.

The old world, too, was brought in to complement the indignation and anger of the new, as heroes of the past who had defended Russian soil made their appearances and the soul of Napoleon, humiliated by his Russian defeat, migrated to Hitler.

Besides literature and history, cartoons were also able to draw on visual formulae, some of very long standing. Some are straightforward visual metaphors, such as sweeping up (as in Heine's picture of a man sweeping up the dead leaves of National Socialism); movement of figures in a picture is immediately seen as an advance of any sort, say ideas or political groups; broken chains stand for freedom regained. An important device is the use of a transformation of one object or person into

'Bufo horribilis Germannicus.'
(Horrible German frog)

This coloured drawing from a private collection may have been for publication. The artist is Robert Sherriffs, film cartoonist for Punch. *It is an example of the theory of Lavater in the eighteenth century that human characters can be understood by observing what animals they resemble. The finishing touch to this caricature of Göring is in the markings on the frog's green skin, aeroplane crosses as well as swastikas.*

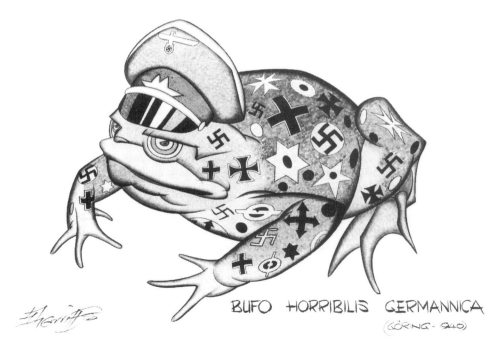

BUFO HORRIBILIS GERMANNICA
(GÖRING · 940)

Flatter

HIS MASTER'S VOICE

(**above**) *Hitler is here depicted listening to his former self, a useful ironic device in art as in literature; the modern touch of the gramophone was the idea of the emigré Austrian-born artist, Joseph Flatter, who lived and worked in London from the mid-thirties. 'Hitler made me an artist,' he wrote; he campaigned relentlessly against Fascism, and became a valued artist for the Ministry of Information, who organized exhibitions of his anti-Fascist cartoons. 'I drew many hundreds of cartoons during the war and, to my surprise, ideas never failed me. . . . The moving force was hatred, it took concrete shape before my eyes. And my hatred of those responsible for the wanton cruelty done to so many innocent victims was boundless. I went about in the shape of my adversaries, I crept into their skin, I "drew, hanged and quartered" them.'*

(**right**) *Walter Trier's drawing of Churchill in a tower of hats makes a witty point about Churchill's accumulation of jobs besides that of Prime Minister. Trier, an emigré artist originally from Prague, was deft at good-humoured characterization, though he was also a successful propaganda cartoonist for* Die Zeitung, *a Ministry of Information paper which was dropped by the RAF into European countries; before arriving in London he had practised as a book illustrator (his best known commission being for Kaestner's* Emil and the Detectives*), and his satirical drawings in the thirties had included work for Simplicissimus.*

something else, the most remarkable examples being in animated film. Medieval images are usable, such as figures of death, or a setting like a chessboard, with its implications of life as a game played well or badly. In Eastern cartoons, demons and evil spirits may appear, as angels and devils do in the West. As for people, the familiar association of character with an animal or bird has been a standby of visual imagery.

Editorial cartoons have explicit meanings, but there is a potent class of cartoon which interests the historian not for its plain narrative, but its underlying implicit assumptions. This is the category of strip cartoons and comic books, not easy to disentangle either from each other or the cartoon films with which they are connected (particularly in the United States of America during the war, and now also in Japan). First, it is true that cartoon characters like Donald Duck or Bugs Bunny went to war for their country; these films were explicitly patriotic. But Donald Duck has a way of life natural enough in his own country, which was equally naturally seen as threatening in Latin America; a classic text on *How to Read Donald Duck*, written in 1971, makes the point.

Strip cartoons sustain the values with which their readers are familiar. For example, everyday life is the staple of 'Blondie'. As a description of policy for the strip explains: 'We stay away from issues on which we have to take sides. We try to make friends, not enemies. Blondie and Dagwood are concerned with eating, sleeping, raising children and making money. We figure if we stick to those four activities, we're bound to hit somebody who can relate to the strip.' A more hostile way of making the same point, by an advocate of political comics, is this: 'They

partly owed their success to the fact that they never sounded the least note of satire or parody, and steered clear of controversy in any form. The comic-strip characters were created to imitate and promote the bourgeois way of life.'

The American way of life had had many admirers in Europe during the thirties, as seen through cartoon strips which were syndicated in European papers. These mainly vanished for the war years. German authorities in various countries attempted to replace American material with more politically acceptable publications, since the importance of children's reading was a point of policy. An even more impressively appealing medium of American influence was also missing – film. A writer on propaganda in 1938, Sidney Rogerson, commented: 'Although this is uncontrolled and dictated solely for commercial profit, it has had a greater effect on the outlook, habits and morals of wide sections of mankind of all races in a short time than any other movement, sociological or religious.'

After the Second World War, American cartoon strips proved to have enduring qualities for success. Syndication returned, though with

---

Al Capp's Li'l Abner strip began in 1934. Before that, Al Capp had drawn for Ham Fisher's Joe Palooka strip, which also featured hillbilly characters. Al Capp's creation of Dogpatch and its inhabitants, though, became by far the most famous hillbilly scene. Li'l Abner was widely syndicated in the American newspapers; but this set of panels was a commercial advertisement in McCall's Magazine. *Marketing cartoon characters has been a profitable modern activity, most visibly by the Disney organization; enlisting cartoon characters in the war was both official, and, as here, commercial practice.*

Hitler and his allies are shown at symbolic sizes, with the phrase 'led by the nose' pictorially expressed. Saul Steinberg was a master of the captionless drawing, much appreciated at the New Yorker. It was with the help of this magazine that he was rescued from US internment as an alien in 1943; he had reached America from his native Roumania after studying architecture in Milan, where his cartooning career began. Steinberg's service in the US Navy included duties in China, North Africa and Italy.

some lesser force where a native comics industry had been built up, as in France. But an international welcome was guaranteed to characters like those of Al Capp. He was once asked whether his characters typified America. He replied: 'I thought so, until I spoke in Stockholm and my audience was stunned to discover that Daisy Mae was not a typical Swedish girl and that Li'l Abner was not the average local lout. And that Senator Phogbound was not a former Prime Minister. But, later, when I went to Brazil, I found the same puzzlement there. All my characters were known by Brazilian names and spoke Portuguese and had been accepted for years as typical Brazilians.'

The cartoon strips of everyday America were complemented by other themes, adventure, crime and the phenomenal success of super-heroes of whom Superman, with his double identity as a workaday journalist, Clark Kent, was the first to appear in the new comic book format in 1937. The psychological sleight of hand in this case was not inventing a powerful figure – Popeye after eating a can of spinach was already that – but making a superman the alternate of a city commuter.

The war thus started with a rich variety of personalities in cartooning. With editorial cartoons an incomplete but interesting history of the war can be compiled. In other cartoons a variety of insights can be gained about the nations in the conflict and their peoples. Besides which, there are excellent drawings and funny jokes. The scope of this short study, then, is mainly within the practice of cartooning, while some sorts of germane drawing, say for graphic design, for historical record, for advertising or as works of art remain on its periphery.

Chapter 2

BRITAIN ALONE

The period in Europe between the two world wars has been called the lost peace. Three Fascist states were created, Italy, Germany and Spain; as the 1930s advanced, it seemed as if war might be the only way to prevent the power of Italy and Germany expanding. The well-meant effort of the founding of the League of Nations was ineffectual. In 1935 Italy invaded Abyssinia, and soon it was Germany's turn.

Germany made a double change in the political map of Europe in 1938. First, Austria was merged with Germany in the spring; secondly, part of Czechoslovakia was ceded to Germany in the autumn. The agreement of Britain, France and Italy was gained by Hitler at a meeting in Munich for this cession of the Sudetenland. A main figure of the negotiation was Neville Chamberlain, the British Prime Minister, who was portrayed in a cartoon in *Punch* as 'A Great Mediator'. The assessment had a short life, since it was contradicted by the subsequent dismemberment of Czechoslovakia. The Sudetenland did become a province of Germany, but in addition Bohemia and Moravia became a German protectorate, Slovakia became precariously independent, and Ruthenia was annexed by Hungary. Fascism had become the most threatening and powerfully placed force in European politics.

Communism was implacably opposed to Fascism. This opposition was vividly expressed by cartoons in Russia, or in anti-Bolshevik material in Germany. In other countries and parties less definite policy lines were taken. In Britain and France, for example, many newspapers were owned by the political right, and as editorial policy usually determined the outlook of a paper's cartoons, fierce opposition to Fascism was rather little in evidence. There was nevertheless some protest and ridicule expressed about the dictators. Evidence can be found in successive editions of a book about Hitler portrayed in caricature round the world, which the German authorities surprisingly were persuaded to publish. It is a notable own goal, and goes to prove that all publicity is not necessarily good publicity.

The increasing likelihood of a major European war was thus not easily predicted from the tone of articles and cartooning in the press. A reluctant and eventually justified prophet of war was David Low, who reacted with sharp dismay to the Munich agreement. Across the Atlantic, premonition of European catastrophe had been the theme of the 1937 Pulitzer prize cartoon by Clarence Batchelor; a prostitute labelled 'War', a skull for a head, makes an invitation to 'Any European Youth' saying: 'Come on in, I'll treat you right. I used to know your Daddy.'

In Germany international affairs were treated with growing confidence. Cartoonists could

TRUTH WILL PREVAIL

The Czechoslovak emigré newspaper in London, in an issue for October, 1939, had this symbolic cartoon. It shows Tomáš Masaryk, first president of the republic, looking down at the dark castle skyline in Prague; in the background are the Eiffel Tower and London Bridge as symbols of hope. The caption is the slogan of Jan Hus, who was burned for heresy in 1415.

Čechoslovák v Anglii

The Czechoslovak in England — Nezávislý týdeník — Independent Weekly

Ročník I. č. 3.   Londýn, 28. října 1939   2d.

28. X. 1939

(**opposite**) *The Russo-German Pact seen through Japanese eyes, using European symbolism of a duel. The pop-gun corks forming a handclasp is a happy invention, at which the globe has good cause to be astonished.*

POLAND GREETS HER GOOD NEIGHBOURS

Arthur Szyk drew this angry cartoon for the left-wing American periodical PM. *Szyk was originally from Poland, had enlisted in the Russian army in 1914, but fought in the Polish army against the Bolsheviks in 1919-20; he then lived in Paris, escaping to Canada in 1940. The drawing was put into his anthology of European anti-Fascist drawings,* The New Order, *published in 1941.*

PAX VOBISCUM
(PEACE BE WITH YOU)

Arthur Szyk's bitter comment on the Russo-German Pact is an admirable example of his meticulous draughtsmanship, which had led him to be chosen to illuminate the Covenant of the League of Nations. Hitler and Stalin are shown holding palms of peace; behind them a soldier hangs on a cross inscribed 'Poland'.

describe their country as increasingly powerful and important – a great contrast with the depressed years of the immediate post-war period. German cartooning was restricted to views acceptable to the National Socialist party. Publishing and especially the newspapers were under political control. By 1938 Hitler could say, 'We have banished the idea that it is any part of political freedom for people to say what they please through the newspapers.'

The mechanics of the control of German publishing were thorough. At the beginning of the century there had been a flourishing provincial press and a wide range of publishers. After the First World War this pattern still existed, incorporating an active Marxist press and a substantial number of publishing houses owned by Jews. A first target of the Nazi party on taking power in 1933 was to destroy this variety. The Marxist press was seized and expropriated. The law was changed to subvert the power of the publishers, in place of whom editors were made responsible for the content of newspapers. In 1935 a further control was imposed through a system of licensing, by which every newspaper was required to apply for a certificate of reliability. One of the few provincial papers to keep something of its original conservative but individual standing was the *Frankfurter Zeitung*, owned by the chemical firm I.G. Farben, whose reprieve was partly due to the argument that it was one of the world's great newspapers which was read with respect abroad.

In such soil no seeds of satire could grow, so that the survival of *Simplicissimus* into the years of the war is a paradox. This journal had been the most brilliant of all European graphic

ABRAHAM AND ISAACS

This strip sequence by von Waldl in Das Schwarze Korps *is an instructive mixture of anti-Semitic and anti-British imagery. The story of Abraham offering to sacrifice his son Isaac is travestied by this narrative in which Britain (as Abraham) does in fact sacrifice other nations for selfish reasons. The SS paper carried both anti-Semitic and some anti-Christian material.*

satirical magazines before 1914, whose pages in the 1920s had sparkled with the provocative talents of George Grosz, as well as the great figures of earlier years. It had passed into decline. Some relics of high standards of draughtsmanship were still kept up, for Olaf Gulbransson and Erich Schilling continued to contribute in the 1940s, but the satire and sharp criticism of German life had gone. For some readers the crucial betrayal of the magazine's real mission had been in 1914, when the staff decided to limit its scope during the First World War to being a patriotic and nationalist paper. The Second World War was a feeble reprise.

Nor was there a welcome for independent editorial cartooning in the press at large. Papers were seen by the Nazi leaders as party organs:

those with the largest circulations were owned by Eher Verlag, the printing and publishing concern responsible for Party material, from best-selling books like Hitler's *Mein Kampf* (My Struggle) to handbills for meetings. *Der Angriff* was a labour front paper from the party's early days, started by Goebbels. It was followed by the purchase of *Völkischer Beobachter*, a small run-down paper which was built up into a massive circulation as a main party vehicle, published both in Berlin and Munich. *Das Reich* became a major weekly, and the paper in which Goebbels himself chose to write; the main illustrated magazine, also with a circulation of more than a million, was *Signal*. More directly bound to the party organizations themselves were such papers as *Das Schwarze Korps*, the paper of the SS, *Die Hitlerjugend* for the Hitler

SAYING GOODBYE
'Today we leave to fight for England and culture, Papa.' 'Good, my son, and when you are over there, remember we have already shed blood for England's money interests.'

A cover for Simplicissimus *by Eduard Thöny in March, 1940 shows something of the envy, as well as the ridicule, which the Empire attracted. Thöny drew from 1896 to 1944 for the magazine, a total of more than 4000 drawings. Captions to Thöny's drawings were not his own, but written by others on the magazine.*

München, 31. März 1940
45. Jahrgang / Nummer 13

30 Pfennig

SIMPLICISSIMUS

VERLAG KNORR & HIRTH KOMMANDITGESELLSCHAFT, MÜNCHEN

Beim Abschied

(E. Thöny)

„Morgen fahren wir ab, Papa, zum Kampf für England und die Kultur!" — „Gut, mein Sohn; und wenn du drüben bist, dann denke dran, daß wir schon einmal für Englands Geldsack geblutet haben!"

Mariannes Blutspender

(Erich Schilling)

Wird sie das viele schwarze Blut auch vertragen?

MARIANNE'S BLOOD TRANSFUSION
'Will she be able to survive all that black blood?'

This example of racist imagery in Simplicissimus *is by Erich Schilling, whose style took some inspiration from early German woodcuts.* Simplicissimus, *like* Punch, *continued to personify nations, as France is here represented by Marianne. Schilling was a strong supporter of the National Socialist party, and committed suicide after Germany's collapse in 1945.*

Youth, and *NS Monatshefte* for Nazi party members and officials.

At the start of the war the only duty of the newspapers was to chronicle the successes of the German army. The beginning was a lightning campaign in Poland in September, 1939. Eighteen days of success were greeted with triumphant victory announcements on the radio, and were the subject of a propaganda film, *Feuertaufe*. The use of panzers to penetrate opposition quickly proved a most successful strategy, notably well executed by a gifted commander, Guderian. Newspaper readers began to be confirmed in their high opinions of the army's professional excellence. National confidence in the army increased in the spring of 1940.

The key to success in the Norwegian campaign was a seaborne attack, aided by parachute troops. Oslo, Bergen, Trondheim and Narvik were captured on 9 April, 1940, in this way. British troops were sent to Norway and took Narvik from the Germans; but the British campaign as a whole failed, and in May the troops were withdrawn. Denmark was also overrun at the same time as Norway was invaded. The powerless Danish king and his government maintained what independence could be managed. In Norway a German sympathizer named Quisling introduced a new noun meaning traitor into European languages when he was installed in power.

The German army also invaded the Netherlands and Belgium on 10 May. The campaign in Belgium was a decisive defeat for the British and French. By 27 May, when the Belgian army surrendered, the British commander, Gort, had already decided that the British Expeditionary

„Findest du nicht auch, Poilu, daß wir ein schönes Bild engster Zusammenarbeit abgeben?!"

THE TANDEM
'Don't you think, Poilu, that we make a fine picture of the closest collaboration?'

This cartoon in Simplicissimus *plays on the theme of France doing Britain's work. Thöny's early popularity before the First World War had been particularly due to his caricatures of philistine military officers, whose uniforms he drew with the knowledge of an expert, since he had been a student of the French military painter, Détaille.*

THE ANGELS OF PEACE DESCEND ON BELGIUM

Low's celebrated cartoon for the Evening Standard *commemorated the invasion in May, 1940; the black angels are headed by Himmler, holding a Gestapo death list, followed by attendants with a whip and a truncheon. This had personal meaning for the cartoonist who believed, correctly as it turned out, that his name was down for execution in the event of a German conquest of Britain.*

Force had to be evacuated, a process which ended on 4 June.

The evacuation from Dunkirk became a legend. A bitterly humiliating defeat was forgotten in relief at so many soldiers being rescued from the beaches – the British official history gave a total of 366,162 Allied troops as having crossed to Britain, and stated that 765 vessels took part in the evacuation. These were not just destroyers and other naval vessels, but included yachts, river ferries and fishing traw-

AFTER TOULON
'Sorry, Guv. but that's all I caught…'

Laval provides Hitler with the remnants of the French fleet from Toulon; a large part of the fleet had been sunk at Mers-el-Kebir by the Royal Navy. The artist Stephen Roth (he did not use his surname) was one of a number of Czech artists in exile in London, where he exhibited with others at the Czech Embassy; and published his cartoons in three collections.

lers. The involvement of civilians was significant, since they spread the idea of gratitude for a deliverance and reinforced the national will to persist in the war. A substantial number of French troops and some Polish forces left north-western France. British cartoons of these events were sombre if thankful, while in Germany it appeared as if British power had finally been broken.

France signed an Armistice on 22 June, 1940. The north of France and the Atlantic coast came under German rule, France south of the Loire was to be governed by Marshal Pétain, whose centre of government at Vichy was to have civil authority over the whole of France. A British attempt to persuade the French government to move to North Africa and fight on was not successful. The French colonial empire accepted Pétain's authority.

From this time the European press was under German control or influence for four years. The thorough system operating in Germany itself was not possible in all the occupied countries, but the public job of the editorial cartoonist could only be carried out in a very limited way, especially so far as the war itself or matters relating to the German occupations were concerned. There were some clandestine publications, and some courage was shown in occasional expressions of independent views, but, in general, independent European cartooning was silenced. In France some attempts were made to establish a degree of German financial control over French publishing, using a familiar method of buyers acting as front men for the Nazi party; and there were those prepared to act as collaborators. As far as Anglo-French relations were concerned, there were several ways in which dormant antipathies against an old enemy could be awakened. Dunkirk was firmly represented by pro-German opinion as being an example of the British being willing to fight to the last Frenchman, and in the following month the destruction of the French fleet by the Royal Navy was felt by many Frenchmen to be a betrayal. Mers-el-Kebir and Oran are names which figure prominently in German propaganda for France.

Kollaborer, c'est être roulé.

Hitler: 'Give me your watch and I will tell you the time.'

Strong feeling against Laval inspired this bitter comment in the Communist clandestine paper, Le Combat, *of which this was the illustrated supplement.*

DONNANT, DONNANT.

Hitler : - *Donné-moi ta montre, je te donnerai l'heure.*

In July, 1940, a cartoon war between Germany and Britain was a part of that wider propaganda war encompassing the press, broadcasting and film which sought both to keep up morale at home and to persuade countries abroad of the justice of a national cause.

Cartoonists ranged against the Axis powers included some of the best draughtsmen of the century, since British and Allied cartoonists had the company of artists driven out of Germany and the European occupied countries. From Germany, George Grosz, John Heartfield, Theodore Heine; from Poland, Arthur Szyk; from Czechoslovakia, Adolf Hoffmeister, Walter Trier and Stephen Roth; from Roumania, Saul Steinberg; Ragvald Blix of *Simplicissimus* returned disconsolate to his native Norway, and then joined Heine in neutral Sweden; Josef Flatter from Austria became an active propaganda cartoonist in Britain. Nor were these cartoonists working in cultural isolation, for there were compatriots especially in London who were actively engaged in the war against Germany; in Britain were the Norwegian King and his government, the Queen of the Netherlands and her government, the Belgian government in exile, the Polish government in exile, and De Gaulle as the leader of the Free French. In the United States there were substantial numbers of European settlers with sympathies in the war. These cartoonists were certainly better placed than the unfortunate artists in Germany who were forbidden to work by law, or the unlucky Jean Sennep, later the distinguished cartoonist of *Figaro*, who was reduced to making acidulous drawings in secret of the Vichy atmosphere which he found unendurably treacherous.

THE FRENCH DICTATOR

A cartoon in the Free French periodical Bir Hakeim *in 1943 shows Laval in Hitler's pocket, another pictorial version of a popular phrase.*

ITALY
TAKES PART
IN THE
ATTACK ON
ENGLAND

HERBLOCK

BUCK BENITO
RIDES AGAIN

*Herblock, a widely
syndicated editorial
cartoonist, here plays off
Hitler and Mussolini
against each other. Italy's
slow entry into the war
(declaring war against
France, for example, only
days before the armistice
with Germany was signed)
is satirized. Mussolini's poor
showing had some economic
justification, as Mussolini's
advisers argued that the
country was not well
enough equipped to go
to war.*

British cartoonists, meanwhile, first of all had to keep the aspidistra flying, at which they were undeniably adept. In the Ministry of Information there were officials who proved to be rather less capable of judging the popular mood than either the cartoonists or the new Prime Minister, Winston Churchill. The fiasco of the Norwegian campaign had brought Churchill to power, and he proved inescapably the man of the hour in his rock-firm willpower, his strong sense of history, his ability for inspiring others, his gift for memorable speeches, and his restless mental energy.

The German leaders hoped that, with France out of the war, the British would be inclined to make peace. Goebbels geared some of his propaganda to the belief that a divided country would throw out Churchill, and in September Hitler made a speech in which he described the uncertainty of Englishmen as to when 'he' was coming. 'Keep calm, "he" will come all right.' But he did not, and he was wrong to think that the British were divided in any way. Low epitomized a national determination with a cartoon of a soldier standing on a map of Britain, fist clenched, defying Hitler's Europe by saying, 'Very well, alone!' This was a feeling that can also be documented extensively in articles, letters and diaries, and was also conveyed by American reporters and broadcasters to their American publics. The German propaganda machine asserted that 'in Britain, the entire population, faced by the threat of invasion, has been flung into a state of complete panic'. The appropriate response was a cartoon by Pont of stolid men in an English public house, phlegmatic and undisturbed, for which this quotation was used as a caption.

'The days for ghosts are over, gentlemen.'

In the Völkisher Beobachter, *in 1940, a German soldier speaks to the shades of Louis XIV, Richelieu and Clemenceau. This image has a long and troubled ancestry in the struggle for European power between Germany and France; the setting in the Hall of Mirrors at Versailles, built by Louis XIV, leading into a room commemorating French victories, was charged with painful meaning for the French. It was used by Bismarck to proclaim his master Wilhelm I as Emperor of Germany after the French defeat in 1871; and, in revenge, was the site chosen by Clemenceau for the signing of the Peace Treaty of Versailles after Germany's defeat in the First World War.*

The man in the street had confidence in the strength of the Royal Navy, and took some comfort in the Channel. For the cartoonists there was also the useful historical memory of an invasion which had failed to materialize, despite Napoleon's threats of conquering Britain. One cartoon reproduced in a wartime book was captioned 'The unchanged menu of Kentishmen for invaders', and the soldiers are seen as having prepared for Napoleon's banquet 'Gunpowder Soup, Force Meat Balls, Kentish Artichoke, and Firework Custard'; cartoons with the figure of Napoleon at Hitler's shoulder made the same point. Churchill's rhetoric was defiant; after asserting the strength of the regular army and the Home Guard, for example, he went on to say, 'Should the invader come to Britain, there will be no placid lying-down of people in submission as we have seen, alas, in other countries. We shall defend every village, every town and every city.'

The need to fight in the streets was prevented by the Royal Air Force, which ensured that no invasion took place. The official dates of the Battle of Britain are given as 10 July–31 October, 1940. Nearly twice as many German

The Punch *cartoonist Pont died prematurely in 1940, but no one was in better control of British understated humour. This deflation of Goebbels' propaganda statement about Britain in 1940 was picked up by the Ministry of Information and used in its turn as propaganda.*

'. . . Meanwhile in Britain the entire population faced by the threat of invasion, has been flung into a state of complete panic . . . etc., etc., etc.'

David Low succeeded in pinpointing a national mood of defiance with this cartoon. The King wrote at the time to his mother: 'Personally, I feel happier now that we have no allies to be polite to and pamper.' Low's style in the 1940s was in full flood, his strong black line printing clearly even on poor wartime paper. His inspiration was nourished by excellent political and military contacts, and his work was well-known abroad, being much syndicated; an exhibition in New York and radio talks added to his reputation as a spokesman for Britain.

'Very well, alone.'

aircraft were destroyed as British. Fighter Command had been successful in attacking the German bombers, even if at the time the figures for German losses were exaggerated. Broadcast claims and counter-claims were the bread and butter of propaganda – the point about planes was that news was very difficult to verify, as opposed to the losses of ships, which were simple to identify, and about which it was more dangerous to make false claims. The Battle of Britain did not receive prominent billing in cartoons partly because it is easier to represent specific events in a cartoon than a series of events or a process. When the *Luftwaffe* ceased to attack British targets, there was no way of knowing whether these attacks had come to an end, or whether it was no more than a respite. By the end of the year, though, it was clear that the battle in the air had been effective. The Battle of Britain was a tonic for British morale. Where there was fear, it had been overcome, and replaced by determination to defeat an enemy whom there was new reason, from the evidence of bombing, to hate.

FROM THE BALTIC TO THE BLACK SEA

The regular medium of the veteran cartoonist Daniel Fitzpatrick was the St Louis Post-Dispatch. *He was appointed in 1913, and retired in 1958. The occasion of this drawing was the German invasion of Russia, a country which Fitzpatrick visualized as a heroic giant, emerging from tanks, guns and the rifles of a united people. Effective use of dramatic scale was one of Fitzpatrick's hallmarks.*

Chapter 3
MOTHER RUSSIA

Independent states in Eastern Europe found 1939 to be a year of disasters. The German attack on western Poland was swiftly followed by a Russian invasion in the east. A public statement announced that the Russian army's advance on 17 September, 1939, was because 'the Soviet Union felt obliged to intervene to protect its Ukrainian and White Russian brothers'. By October Polish resistance had ceased and Russian forces occupied the eastern half of the country. Poland remained partitioned for the rest of the war. The former government which had fled to Roumania was interned and a government in exile was established in London.

Polish culture lived for the rest of the war in a half light; in the occupied country, east and west, foreign rule prevented any indigenous expression of Polish views. Then came wholly German occupation, with terrible consequences for the population, especially Poland's Jews. Finally Poland was made a battlefield. Escaped Poles fought sometimes as individuals, sometimes in Polish units in other countries' forces. From abroad a faint if definite and defiant Polish voice could be heard.

Russia occupied an area which had been agreed in advance by a Russo-German Pact, made between Stalin and Ribbentrop as Hitler's emissary on 23 August, 1939. The Russian view was that the territory was within an ethnic line in Poland. British opinion was specially

GOEBBELS

In Russian cartoons considerable play was made with Goebbels' short stature, as in this example by Kukryniksy, which also satirizes his domination of German broadcasting. In another Russian cartoon Goebbels is being held like a doll by a soldier, with a caption explaining that this is a full-length portrait of the Propaganda Minister.

'Onward to Moscow!'

This jeering cartoon about Hitler's failure to take Moscow is by Kukryniksy in 1942. The military drum has a long history, and is a useful symbol of vainglory (here it is inscribed with the words 'lightning war'). The German style of marching, the goose step, was adopted in Russia at the time of the Russo-German Pact.

incensed by what was seen as a cynical use of Poland's helplessness; but Russia's opportunity had only arisen because of the failure of the French and the British to agree with Russia on a common policy.

For an international public, an alliance between Communism and Fascism was bewildering. Leading intellectuals and left-wing sympathizers of Russia were in a dilemma. In Britain, David Low was shocked, since he had been arguing for Britain to establish closer relations with the Soviet Union; he saw Russia (together with America) as the long-term hope for the defeat of Germany. He drew what he described as the bitterest cartoon of his life, called 'Rendezvous' where Hitler, as the 'Bloody Assassin of the Workers', meets Stalin as the 'Scum of the

Earth' in a war-stricken scene symbolizing Poland.

Propaganda organizations in Germany and Russia also had their difficulties. In Germany strident anti-Bolshevik propaganda was stopped dead, including military songs which were banned from broadcasting; press instructions about the volte-face were given to put the pact into a historical perspective: 'The decision represents a sensational turning-point in the relations between the two nations and is a return to the traditional co-operation in German-Russian policies'; furthermore, 'no reference, either positive or negative must be made to the ideological differences between the two states... The tone of the comments must be matter of fact and sober. The reader must get neither a feeling of triumph nor of unease *(Schadenfreude)* from it.' In Russia an effort was made to place Germany in a more favourable light; German literature was available, concerts of German music were promoted, and Sergei Eisenstein was diverted from his film career to direct a production of Wagner in Moscow.

The next Russian moves were in the Baltic, where the pact had placed Latvia and Estonia in the Russian sphere of influence. Military control was established there and in Lithuania, the third Baltic state to disappear in 1939. But Finland refused Russian demands, and war was declared. An Anglo-French expedition was planned to help the Finns, for which British landings in Norway were intended as a prelude; in the event only a few volunteers ever reached Finland, and the British and French governments were further discredited. The uneven contest was over when Finland made peace on 12 March, 1940. From the summer of 1940 to the spring of 1941 the Russo-German Pact held. Germany drew three countries, Slovakia, Hungary and Roumania, into the Axis alliance with Italy and Japan. Italy embarked on a war with Greece; Germany began by invading Yugoslavia to support Italy in Greece. Yugoslavia, like Czechoslovakia, was dismembered.

Hitler intended, in due course, to attack Russia. It was a master plan which fitted with Nazi ideology about the superiority of the Aryan race, and the destiny of Germany to achieve great power and possessions. The attack was brought nearer by fear for German supplies being under future threat from Russia, whether Swedish ore or Roumanian oil. There was also the unexpected fact of Britain's continued stand, despite German domination

Es ist angerichtet . . .

Zeichnung: Bogner

Die Bürger Moskaus sind bereit, für Stalin durchs Feuer zu gehen

IT IS ALL IN ORDER
'The citizens of Moscow are ready to go through fire for Stalin.'

This cartoon by Bogner from Das Schwarze Korps *in 1941 appeared in the successful phase of Germany's attack on Russia, when it seemed that Moscow would be captured. Stalin is seen setting fire to the city, while he retreats. In historical fact, administrative government was moved out of the capital, but soon returned. Stalin himself stayed in the Kremlin.*

of Europe. Hitler decided on a pre-emptive strike, calculating that, after Russia's defeat, Britain would make peace, and America refrain from entering the European war. Three German armies invaded Russia on 22 June, 1941.

The differences in ideology between fascism and communism again became important, instead of being suppressed as they had been during the time of the Russo-German Pact. Germans were reminded that the Russians were to be feared, like other Slavs, as sub-humans (*Untermenschentum*). Confidence could be felt in the German army with its proved success in spectacular victories in Europe. The propaganda ministry's line was that a short and decisive campaign in Russia could be expected.

The initial German advance into Russia was a triumph, but fell short of Hitler's aim at a decisive victory. Three German armies drove forward to Smolensk, towards Leningrad and to Kiev. In August Hitler decided to halt the central army, which was to wait for the two armies on the wings to defeat their opponents, after which the armies would unite in an attack on Moscow. But Leningrad was never taken. In the south there were substantial victories, the Ukraine, most of the Crimea and the Donetz basin being occupied.

HOME IN FRITZLAND
'Father used to drink beer, mother coffee, and me tea. We all have the same tastes now.'

Ganf's cartoon from Krokodil *was one of those chosen for an album of humorous articles and drawings published in Britain in 1943. At this date the assertion of severe hardship for German civilians was still wishful thinking.*

Although the central German army under von Bock reached the outskirts of Moscow, he advised Hitler that his men were at exhaustion point, and the attack was broken off. For Russia this was a propaganda point gained, making a scornful comparison of Hitler with Napoleon, who had captured Moscow, more convincing.

German victory in the south did not bring the benefits which had been anticipated for two reasons: the Russians had a scorched-earth policy, leaving little of value behind them; they also achieved an extraordinary feat by moving industry out of the Ukraine to the east, where new industrial plants were built up which eventually outmatched German production. More than twelve million people are said to have taken part in this unprecedented transfer of industry, by which Germany lost the war of resources.

From the first day of the invasion the Russian press concentrated on a war of opinion against Fascism and the German leaders. The Russo-German Pact became a historical event which had been needed to enable Russia to have breathing space before an inevitable conflict. Russia was a country transformed by war into a land not only of Socialism, but once again sacred soil, Mother Russia, formerly defended by heroes of the past, whose ghosts were invoked in cartoons and posters. Napoleon's defeat and retreat from Moscow were recalled. Historical parallels were also pointed out in films, including those by Eisenstein.

The Russian press was dominated by official publications, of which *Pravda* and *Izvestia* were newspapers with the largest circulations in the world. Cartoons in these papers were vehement and emphatically drawn, using the

FAMILY PORTRAITS
'All my three children are pilots, snipers, army doctors…'
'Are these their portraits?'
'No – their husbands' portraits.'

This cartoon by K. Rotov appeared in Krokodil, *neatly making its point about women in Russian society. Rotov drew for* Krokodil *from 1923, and for* Pravda *from 1928. He was also well-known for children's book illustrations.*

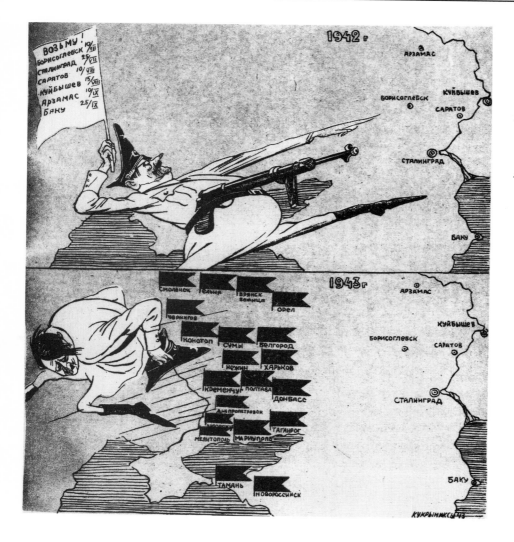

This cover for Krokodil *is a
before-and-after image, a
simple but effective way of
presenting the contrast
between Hitler's arrogant
advance into Russia in
1942, and his retreat in the
following year.*

sort of thick line for which Low was known. Deni was a notably effective political cartoonist for *Pravda* in this vein. He was also a poster artist. Other major cartoonists such as Moor, Orlov, Lebedov, Semenov and Efimov too worked in both media. The role of a graphic artist in the Soviet Union was well defined in giving expression to socialist principles and their application.

In Communist theory there was a distinction which came from a pamphlet written by Lenin in 1902, 'What is to be done?' This text quotes a sentence by the nineteenth-century writer Plekhanov: 'A propagandist presents many ideas to one or a few persons; an agitator presents only one or a few ideas, but presents them to a mass of people.' Lenin glossed this sentence by describing the agitator as rousing discontent and indignation against injustice, while explanations are left to the propagandist. The complementary activities of arousing emotions and giving explanations were given administrative form in the 1930s in an organization which combined them, *Agitprop*. Most Russian posters and cartoons are agitation; during the war there was a single and dominant idea, that the German army must be defeated; the means through which this idea is to be conveyed was a secondary matter.

The team of artists who called themselves Kukryniksy are exemplary. They had worked alongside each other since the 1920s, when they were students together at the School of Arts and Crafts in Moscow. Their wide graphic practice included posters, cartoons, illustrations and paintings. During the war they designed about two hundred posters and stencils for posters, besides drawing cartoons for *Pravda*, *Izvestia*, *Krokodil* and other publications. Several of their posters were reprinted in Britain, having been brought back by Lord Beaverbrook from his visit to Russia in 1941; one of these showed a Russian and a British airman, both in planes over Berlin, bombs falling, with the slogan: 'Meeting over Berlin. The brother-nations arranged a rendezvous over the enemy's town. This handshake will not be healthy for the Germans.'

Their aim as agitators through cartooning was quite explicit: 'We aim at arousing in the

'I have lost my little ring, and in the ring were twenty-two divisions.'

Hitler, as a poor old woman who has lost a ring, is Kukryniksy's way of describing the eventual Russian victory at Stalingrad. The map shows the city, and within a red line is the surrendered German army represented by swastikas.

Red Army, and among the workers on the Home Front, wrath and contempt for the enemy. We aim at amusing them, because what can raise the spirit like wholesome laughter?...From day to day we brand and expose and ridicule the enemy in hundreds of cartoons, for that is how we understand the artist's and satirist's task in wartime.' The means with which they achieved their aim was through a forceful line, sometimes enhanced by a brilliant visual metaphor, as in the noose forming the number six in 1946 above the heads of the defendants in the Nuremberg trials.

One serious problem of publications of any sort in Russia was how they could be distributed. Another difficulty was finding a medium through which the peoples of Russia of every nationality and level of education could be reached. Two solutions had been found in the early years of the new state; *Agitprop* trains brought new art and information to people in many different areas; and as for posters, a central production of stencils enabled them to be copied in every centre to which they had been sent. The name for these stencils was at first ROSTA but in the Second World War they had been taken over by the official Russian news agency and they were termed TASS windows. A typical TASS window dealing with the war was a vilification of Nazi leaders, with an insulting or sarcastic text. They had a valued place in Russian traditions, gaining some of their power from association with peasant woodcuts and popular art; Mayakowski, the poet of the Revolution, had been an effective writer for this sort of poster.

The main vehicle of satirical humour was *Krokodil*. A British anthologist of the magazine writing in 1943 compared it with *Punch*, *The New Yorker*, *Le Rire* and *Simplicissimus*. The comparison is not altogether apt since *Krokodil* had a larger circulation, and so was not as restricted in its type of audience. During the war the magazine was published on eight pages (four sheets) in colour, although many of the joke cartoons were in black and white. The covers were often dramatic, with an authoritative weight of commentary on the war situation. In 1943, for example, a cover shows two maps — Hitler in 1942 striding into Russia, and in 1943 cowering back; another shows Hitler as a burst pipe along the war frontier. The images in *Krokodil* are frequently violent, with soldiers using rifle butts or bayonets, and in 1945 there is even a drawing of Hitler, Mussolini and Hirohito skewered on a bayonet. In the Russian cartoon war it was a fight to the death, and the grim issue of survival lies behind the images.

One of the *Krokodil* covers was about the major drama of the southern front, the battle for Stalingrad in 1942. Hitler particularly wanted to capture the city as a symbolic humiliation for the Russian leader. It has been described as a battle of attrition, like Verdun in the First World War, and it attracted widespread coverage in cartoons round the world. It was a bitter battle, fought in the streets, but the Red Army was never completely ousted. In September Hitler went so far as to assert in a speech: 'The capture of Stalingrad will be completed, and you may be sure that no one will ever drive us out of this place again.' By November the Russians were in a position to mount a counter-attack, and succeeded in cutting off the German Sixth Army under Paulus, who himself surrendered with his army.

Goebbels faced a painful difficulty in deciding how to treat the news; at a mass meeting in Berlin he chose to speak in a vein of heroic fiction, describing how the heroes of Stalingrad had listened to the Fuehrer's proclamation on 30 January, 1943, of the tenth anniversary of the Nazi régime, then 'sung the national anthem with raised arms with us, perhaps for the last time in their lives...What an attitude for German soldiers in this great time... Stalingrad was and is Fate's great call of alarm to the German nation.' The clear implication was that these heroic soldiers had died for their country, and more than 90,000 prisoners of war were not mentioned; it was from the Russian broadcasting service in German that relatives could know their names and addresses.

Radio treatment of the German disaster was

grandiloquent in its mourning, one way of avoiding a sober assessment of defeat. The consequences of defeat were soon felt, however, in the conscription of men and women for war work, to gain victory in what was now described as the 'total war' being waged. This phrase was placarded above the platform for a mass rally at the Sport Palace in Berlin on 18 February, 1943, a highlight of Goebbels' career. He described the atmosphere as he posed a question to the audience: 'At this question the Sport Palace experiences a demonstration the like of which even this old scene of the fight of National Socialism has only seen on special peak events of our national life. The masses jump from their seats as if electrified. A "Yes" from thousands of voices rages like a hurricane through the wide round hall. What the participants of this

'Two calendars. German lies, Soviet victories.'

This cartoon by Boris Efimov contrasts the German and Russian calendars for the summer of 1943. The German plan included a decisive attack against the Red Army, and surrounding Moscow. As Goebbels accompanies Hitler on a wrecked Tiger tank, he mouths weasel words, 'elastic defence'. The superiority of Russian armaments is made particularly clear.

demonstration experience is a national vote and an expression of will power, which could not be expressed more spontaneously.'

The other legendary city of the war in Russia was Leningrad. It was besieged from the first year of the invasion in 1941, and was not relieved until 1944. As in the south, industrial plant was evacuated to safer locations. The sole military objective was to hold out as long as possible, for which purpose a road behind the city across the ice was a precarious lifeline. Tyranny and brutality in Russia in the thirties had ensured overt and concealed opposition to Stalin's rule, which had caused the Russian commander Vlasov to surrender his army in front of Leningrad to the Germans in the hope of being able to lead them against Stalin. The inhabitants of Leningrad were never free of the fear of the city's capture; they did not know of their attackers' difficulties. A factor in the aggressive character of Russian cartooning was a believed need to maintain a greater fear of the Germans than of the known and desperate conditions in which Russians lived, for example in Leningrad, and thus to avoid further desertions or surrender.

Merciless brutality on the German side against Slav people who were regarded in Nazi ideology as sub-human confirmed the validity of the Russian cartoonists' attacks. The scale of this brutality was not known until later, but evidence was plentiful enough in the war to make hatred of Germany prevail in Russian public opinion.

After the surrender of Paulus' army at Stalingrad in 1943, and the subsequent major tank battle at Kursk in the summer, Russian cartoons had more reason for an optimistic tone; but generally they remained aggressive and vindictive. Gleeful images of the downfall of Mussolini, and gloating pictures of Hitler's discomforture are to be found in *Krokodil*. Imaginative fantasy had a little more play, perhaps, as in the work of Boris Efimov.

The number of Russians who died in the war, however, continued to remain tragic. Little direct military assistance came to Russia from her allies. Arctic convoys from Britain started badly in 1942, in particular with the destruction of convoy PQ17 which was dispersed on what later proved to have been a false alarm; some supplies reached Russia through Persia. Help of another sort, creating a second front by an invasion of France, was the remedy urged by Russia on her allies.

November, 1943, saw a conference of Stalin, Roosevelt and Churchill at Teheran. The European invasion was at last agreed. This important conference spotlights the advantage that the Allied powers had through their ability to co-ordinate a policy, which had been quite absent in the conduct of the war by Germany, Italy and Japan. It also stresses the personal significance of the war leaders, confirming the roles that they are shown as playing in the war seen through cartoons.

The future of Poland was discussed at Teheran, but not decided. A new problem was created by the German disclosure of the bodies of 4000 Polish officers buried at Katyn. They were claimed by Goebbels to have been Russian victims.

Chapter 4

THE GREAT EAST ASIA WAR

Japan during the 1930s was an expanding power in Asia. In 1931 the army dragged political leaders into an invasion of Manchuria, which was to be added to the two existing colonies of Korea and Taiwan. The Japanese established a puppet state of Manchukuo in Manchuria. In 1937 the war against China began again; by the end of that year both Shanghai and Nanking, the capital of Chiang Kai-shek's government had been captured. In 1938 the Wu-han cities on the Yangtse were taken as well as Canton, the main Chinese port in the south. The Chinese government's headquarters, however, had moved out of Japanese reach to Chungking. Russia became anxious about the extension of Japanese power, and intervened to save Chungking; but in September, following the Russo-German Pact, an armistice was agreed between Russia and Japan.

International feeling against Japan's war in China was widespread, and took a new form in 1939. The United States had provided much of Japan's war supplies, but announced that the arrangements under which they had been imported – a treaty of 1911 – would come to an end in six months. During 1940 negotiations with the United States over steel and oil became more difficult, even more so after Japan occupied bases in south-east Indo-China by agreement with the French Vichy government. Japan could not obtain oil either from the United States or the Dutch East Indies. This was seen as a threat to Japan both by the military leaders and the hitherto more moderate naval leadership. In September, 1941, it was agreed that understanding must be reached with the United States within a few weeks, or Japan would declare war on America and Britain.

The war party in Japan was strong, and, because of the success achieved in the Chinese war, little opposed. Japanese scholars have termed the period between 1931 and 1941 *kurai tanima* (the dark valley) for its excessive nationalism, which was unhappily expressed in militarism and violence. Any possible political balance in the country had been destroyed by the elimination of radical and left-wing parties, leaving a nation which apparently only thought in one patriotic way. The executions so necessary in Germany to maintain unanimity of opinion were not needed in Japan, where social pressures and re-education were used to enforce conformity.

The press formed part of this conformist unity. The National Mobilization law of 1938, and a drastic law controlling discussion, publication, assembly and organization in 1941 ensured compliance. The press, although financially strong, was politically weak. News was available through Domei, a national news agency. Supervision of the press was exercised by a Cabinet Information Committee. The

TERRY AND THE PIRATES

Milton Caniff was fulfilling the wish of the editor of the New York Daily News for a strip cartoon 'based on a blood and thunder formula, carrying a juvenile angle, and packed with plenty of suspense.' It started in October, 1934, with the oriental setting which continued through the war. Another popular strip was not so fortunate. 'Fu Manchu' presented the Chinese in such an unfavourable light, so the Chinese government felt, that the cartoon was stopped.

THE ASSASSIN STRIKES

The Japanese air attacks on Pearl Harbor, Hawaii, and on Clark Field in the Philippines were commemorated in this cartoon by Fitzpatrick for the St Louis Post-Dispatch, *published on 8 December, 1941. A bloody dagger, a cloak, and identity established by the emblem on the sleeve are economical elements for conveying emotions felt at the outbreak of war.*

result was that the newspapers mainly reported official announcements. Further, the number of newspapers was greatly reduced, partly by mergers, and partly through a policy by which only one newspaper was permitted to each prefecture.

The domestic situation in the United States was entirely different. In a politically divided country, President Roosevelt was in no position to carry out a war policy even if he had wished it. Strong voices for isolationism had urged him to keep out of the war in Europe, and war in the Pacific declared by America would have raised a storm. Japan's attack on Pearl Harbor was possibly the only start to the war which could have received such overwhelming national support in the United States. However, although the attack was unexpected, a possible war with Japan did not seem far away in the work of one cartoonist, Milton Caniff. He was one of the top group of highly paid strip-cartoonists in America, whose reputations were greatly boosted by their work appearing in newspapers across the country.

The pattern of newspaper production in the United States was regional, but feature writers and strip-cartoonists, whose work had beneficial effects on newspaper sales, marketed their material through agencies. These agencies were comparable with the distribution networks of cinemas; their products were similarly popular, and an integral part of the cultural climate of the country. Caniff had started *Terry and the Pirates* as an adventure strip cartoon for the *Chicago Daily News* in October, 1934. Terry was a pilot whose adventures were in the East. By 1937 the Japanese war with China had filtered into the strip, with the Japanese as 'the invaders'. After Pearl Harbor, Terry remained for some months a civilian, but then joined the US Army Air Corps, his hero being Colonel Flip Corkin, who gave the newly commissioned Terry some advice:

You'll get as angry as the Devil at the army and its so-called red tape...but be patient with it...somehow the old eagle has managed to end up in possession of the ball in every war since 1776 – so humor it along... Okay, sport, end of speech...When you get in that 'Wild Blue Yonder' the song talks about – remember, there are a lot of good guys missing from mess tables in the South Pacific, Alaska, Africa, Britain, Asia and back home who are sorta counting on you to take it from here! Good night, kid!

These extracts are from a Sunday page published on 17 October, 1942, which a Congressman suggested was 'deserving of immortality' and was consequently read into the Congressional Record. Meanwhile, back at the front, soldiers were reading a strip cartoon specially done for them by Caniff, with close attention paid to a blonde called Burma, who had featured in *Terry and the Pirates*. Then this variant strip was given its own name, *Male Call*, whose dark-haired heroine was Miss Grace. Caniff's special abilities were generally recognized in his profession, especially his care with authentic backgrounds including modern technology, whether boats, planes or weapons. His sharp drawing style fitted into striking compositions which used solid black to contrast with open white areas, and his dialogue was persuasive.

A B C D

The letters on the ship's bridge stand for America, Britain, China and the Netherlands (Dutch) in this cartoon from Manga *in 1942 by Ikeda Eiji. The three figures of oppression are Churchill, Roosevelt and Chiang Kai-shek.*

REST CURE

One of his characters was a nurse called Taffy; a critic has commented that she was 'one of the best arguments for a girl becoming an Army nurse that could have been put across by anyone'.

Another recruiting agent for the American forces was the strip cartoonist Ham Fisher. His famous boxer, Joe Palooka, decided to enlist a year before Pearl Harbor. Palooka is portrayed as a gentle giant. The same critic, Coulton Waugh, himself a cartoonist, had the character in clear focus:

(**above**) *This panel cartoon by George Baker typifies the appeal of the Sad Sack. Baker had worked for Walt Disney before joining the army in 1941. The Sad Sack appeared first in* Yank *in May, 1942, and then in* Stars and Stripes. *It became a newspaper comic strip after the war, and a film was made about the character in which Jerry Lewis starred.*

(**right**) *Joe Palooka was the invention of Ham Fisher, who began the strip in 1928. He was himself responsible for the story, but he employed others for drawing, including Al Capp. Both cartoonists had a success during the war, to which their characters were patriotically committed.*

A new, gentle, quiet, strong message tapped day by day and strip by strip into their hearts: race does not matter to Palooka; to Palooka all of you are equal in the right to live and love and have a good time. Comfortable, lazy Palooka, wolfing down a whole chicken out of the icebox in the middle of the night: he would like everybody to be able to do that. Palooka, not so easy-going when someone steps on a pal's right to a good time (and all decent people are pals to him); the quick anger and intensity of his fierce resentment, and then when he had taught the mean one a lesson, somehow they would always end up good friends.

Millions of Americans read the Palooka strip and sympathized with his point of view. Nor was Palooka to be tempted by rank, replying to his young sister at the family farm when saying goodbye: 'No, I ain't gonna be a officer, Rosie; jist a buck private. I don't deserve t'be an'don't know enuff t'be.'

Despite pressure from the Army, Fisher refused to let his character be used as a way of explaining the Officer Cadet School. But Fisher was given army tours, and the accuracy of his strip went with improved army morale. After Pearl Harbor Joe Palooka went to Europe, helped the French underground, served in North Africa and took part in the Normandy invasion. Special qualities of the strip are the quiet sense of Palooka's comment on the issues of the war, and his straightforward gratitude for help, 'Thank-you'.

Another strip cartoon had its origins in problems of naval recruitment. During the 1930s there was difficulty in recruiting for the navy in the landlocked mid-American states, as an admiral complained to a former Lieutenant-Commander, Frank Martinek. Don Winslow was the naval hero of books by Martinek, and the admiral's remark made him think of trying to reach a wider audience. A comic strip seemed the answer, and by good luck he soon afterwards met two artists, Leon Beroth and Carl Hammond. Together they formed a team, and produced *Don Winslow of the Navy*. Carl Hammond joined up, but the other two continued the feature for the last three years of the war. Incidentally, there were other strips for the other services, for example Smilin' Jack was a rival of Terry in the air, and Captain Yank stood for the US Marines; but Don Winslow was unique in being prompted by recruiting needs before the war.

MC NAUGHT SYNDICATE, INC

American entry into the war was followed by the establishment of the Office of War Information, but the scope of this office was not at all comparable with European controls. Nor were the needs of the American government and the public similar. For civilians in the United States, the war was remote, involving neither fighting on American soil nor the bombing of American cities. Only six thousand American civilians died in the war. Industrial production, war savings, saving energy and growing food were typical topics for public campaigns. It was a sign of the American times that when Donald Duck was drafted to help the war effort, one of the films in which he featured was designed to explain to the American taxpayer how helpful paying taxes on time would be to the government. Walt Disney used his talents and the production facilities of his studios for other projects, including some anti-Nazi films, such as *Der Führer's Face* in 1942, and a spectacular promotional film called *Victory through Air Power*. Warner Brothers ought to be mentioned in the context of cartoon films for propaganda

purposes. Bugs Bunny appears in a film called *You're a Sap, Mr Jap*, providing grenades in ice cream cones to unsuspecting Japanese. As in Britain, animated film was partly used for conveying information, and it was in a mixed type of film combining animation with live-action that Disney developed some of his techniques used after the war.

Editorial cartoonists for American papers were well placed to take an overall view of the European war, and very telling some of these cartoons were. They naturally responded fiercely to the attack on Pearl Harbor, and the Pacific became a major area of the newspapers' concern. The veteran cartoonist of the *St Louis Post-Dispatch*, Daniel Fitzpatrick, was one of the most forceful and dramatic cartoonists, good at indicating the relative importance of issues with an armoury of weapons including making figures gigantic and minute. Fitzpatrick's home base was workers' America, the waterfront rather than suburbia; his bleak outlook on international affairs was proved to be well justified by the leaders of the Axis powers

Contour Map (Note Magnetic Azimuths and Topographic Features)

YOU MEAN YOU WANT A GAG, TOO?

JANE

(**above**) *The most famous British strip cartoon was originated and drawn throughout the war by Norman Pett. This episode is from November, 1944, in a story called 'Behind the Lines'. It is her clumsy boyfriend Georgie-Porgie who has managed to rip her dress, the sort of misfortune for Jane that her readers eagerly expected.*

CONTOUR MAP

Milton Caniff's Miss Lace in his strip for the US Army appeared under the title of Male Call.

against whom some of his fiercest cartoons were directed.

A cartoonist of equal celebrity was Rube Goldberg, whose reputation had been made with humorous panel drawings and cartoon strips, notably *That's Life* and *Professor Butts*. In the early 1930s he tried his hand at an ideal character Doc Wright, with whom he became bored; it stopped in 1934, with 100 papers running it. He then lost his audience, attempted a character called Lala Palooza, which was parodied by Ham Fisher with Joe Palooka. He had a spell of not drawing at all; then in 1938 the *New York Evening-Sun* invited him to be their editorial cartoonist, providing three cartoons a week. Heavy line cartooning was not Goldberg's ideal medium, for he had been more at home with a thin pen line and the chance to employ his wit in characteristic detailing of American life. He rightly saw that 'The successful cartoonist deals principally in emotions. His work cannot be pleasing to everyone. Editorial cartooning is essentially destructive. It is an art

'Make fortune by co-operating with Japan.'

A propagandist drawing typical of the psychological warfare used by the Japanese in their attempt to establish the 'Greater East Asia Co-prosperity Sphere'. The scornful reference to the collapse of British power in Asia is typical; but the promise of Japanese co-operation in foreign business proved to be largely illusory.

of protest.' He was himself capable of piercing protest, as in a cartoon about the price of peace paid by using the atomic bomb; it elicited this comment from E.H. Gombrich: 'For one brief moment we seem to see our predicament, face-to-face, as it were, in this nightmare picture which persuades us of its reality.' The image was of a suburban house perched on a bomb balanced on the edge of a precipice.

Japanese defeat was far away in December, 1941, when the destruction of much of the American fleet signalled the start of the Japanese and American conflict in the Pacific. At the same time the Clark airfield in the Philippines was attacked. The Japanese public were dazzled by a run of military successes. Japan transformed the map of South-East Asia. The next hundred days gave Japan the main prizes. Hong Kong was taken in December. Then Singapore, the British fortress wrongly thought to be impregnable from land, surrendered to a Japanese force inferior in number to the British defenders. By the end of April, 1942, Dutch Indonesia had surrendered. The American commander in the Philippines, MacArthur, fought a holding action at Corregidor in the peninsular of Bataan, but was ordered to hand over his command; his successor, Wainwright, had surrendered by 6 May; and by the end of April, 1942, British forces had been driven out of Burma.

This series of striking Japanese victories was a devastating blow to the reputation of the British, whose empire never regained its prestige.

This is a colourful portrayal of malevolent British influence in Asia. Japanese folk literature has a wide variety of spooks, devils, demons and ghosts from which to draw inspiration for narrative images. In this case the devil dressed in a Union Jack is a deep green.

At first Japan was welcomed for a policy which encouraged the independence of Asian states. In time this good will was lost by the arrogance of Japanese administrators – for example in Burma, supposedly an independent state, where the Japanese army interfered in internal affairs.

Australia's part in the Pacific war looked at first as if it would begin with a defence against invasion. There was talk of holding a Brisbane line across the continent. The gloom began to be dispelled soon after the arrival in Australia of MacArthur. No invasion materialized. Australian troops were recalled from the Mediterranean to take part in the war for New Guinea. MacArthur's American and Australian command was in place to recover the islands of Asia, not least the Philippines, which he had left with the words 'I

shall return' (the tidied up version of what he had actually said, 'I have come through and I will return').

The tide that turned first was that of the naval war. Between 4 and 6 June, 1942, in the Battle of Midway, four Japanese aircraft carriers were sunk, decisively changing the prospects of the American fleet for the better. It is an indication of the militarist control of the Japanese press that this significant defeat was reported in the papers as a Japanese victory. By a bizarre chance, the American public was not much better informed. A journalist for the *Chicago Tribune*, Stanley Johnston, not obliged to submit his work to the naval censors, succeeded in piecing together an accurate account of the Japanese vessels concerned (with the aid of *Jane's Fighting Ships*). He was investigated by a grand jury for espionage. It was later disclosed that the US Navy had succeeded in breaking the Japanese codes, and feared that Johnston's report from hearsay and inspired guesswork would be taken by the Japanese as evidence that their codes were being read. Even in 1943 it was said that Americans had the battles of the Coral Sea and Midway confused.

Admiral Nimitz was responsible for the eventual withdrawal of the Japanese from Guadalcanal, where they had intended to build an air base. This hard-fought battle began with forces of 6,000 on each side which swelled to 44,000 Allied troops against 22,500 Japanese. Japanese deaths were estimated at more than four times the Allied killed and wounded, excluding casualties from disease. The battle, which included naval as well as land engagements, finished in February, 1943.

MacArthur was the leader responsible for the Australian victory in New Guinea, where improvisation was the key to success. The campaign there and in Borneo were the main theatres in which the Australian forces were engaged, and which thus attracted the attention of the Australian press. In Australia cartooning had a long and distinguished history. The remarkable Norman Lindsay, veteran of the First World War, was still living, and his powerful imagery continued to have its former power to shock and disturb. Lindsay was staff cartoonist for the *Sydney Bulletin*; almost matching his denunciatory images of the German Kaiser in the First World War, he caricatured the Japanese Emperor as an overdressed and undersized Mikado, owing something to

'**Once again the Tommies have got the boot from behind.**'

This cartoon by Truetsch appeared on the front page of Das Schwarze Korps, *in February, 1942.*

(**right**) *This strip cartoon sequence shows Chiang Kai-shek at the point of defeat in the boxing ring; Churchill and Roosevelt come to his aid, but are defeated by a Japanese hero. The outcome is cheered by black Americans, but dismays the white audience.*

the burlesque treatment of Gilbert and Sullivan's opera.

The daily press in Australia also had its cartoonists, of whom Alex Gurney was memorable for his army pair of Bluey and Curley in the *Melbourne Sun*. The paper whose circulation rose most steeply during the war, however, was *Smith's Weekly*. This campaigning paper had successfully fought for the rights of veterans of the First World War, in particular the maimed and the wounded. The Second World War saw its popularity grow greatly from a circulation of around 50,000 to a quarter of a million.

The history of New Zealand in the war was one of fragile independence, maintained for the most part by the strength of her allies. New Zealand, like Australia, had sent troops to the war in North Africa and the Mediterranean. After Pearl Harbor, New Zealand had only a Home Guard as a defence against invasion (though it was of a formidable size, at 120,000 men). The first American reinforcements arrived in the summer of 1942.

Gordon Minhinnick is a figure to pick out from New Zealand's cartoonists. His newspaper was the *New Zealand Herald*, but his work was syndicated, so his cartoons were seen round the country. Minhinnick was an admirer of Low; his thick line, populist appeal and clearly but forcibly expressed arguments all owe something to his mentor. Minhinnick invented a representative New Zealand character in old soldier Sam; but Minhinnick diffidently felt that he was a 'figure of fun and a convenient mouthpiece' rather than a character in his own right. Old soldier Sam was a favourite with New Zealand servicemen, sharing his popularity with Fred Clueless, a character invented by a young staff

OLD SOLDIER SAM – CANNON FODDER

artist for the *NZEF Times*, Neville Colvin.

American troops serving in the Pacific also had their own papers, among them *Yank* and *Stars and Stripes*. The cartoons in these papers, however, were rarely local in flavour. George Baker wrote a narrative strip for *Yank*, and explained why his character, the Sad Sack, was seen in an army unit anywhere: 'Since the Sad Sack appeared in all the editions, it was necessary to keep the ideas general so that they would have the same response whether it was read by a man in the Aleutians, China, Europe, or, for that matter, Washington. The ideal type of ideas for the Sack's purpose was one in which any soldier seeing it could recall or visualize the same thing happening in his own particular unit. There were, of course, many ideas I used that were applicable only to a certain theatre, but these I tried to broaden enough to be understood anywhere.'

Another army character, this time from *Stars and Stripes*, was the creation of Dave Breger, based on how he felt himself when he enlisted. Breger quoted this description in *Time* approvingly: 'Private Breger is a wide-eyed, over-spectacled, freckled little soldier clumsy, meek, confused, but undismayed. Cartoonist Breger likes to think of "Private Breger" as typical of all the nation's millions of little men to whom soldiering is alien, but who cheerfully acquiesced when war came.' An unusual feature of Breger's cartoons is his way of drawing military ranks; he drew officers larger than enlisted men, enhanced their insignia, made their chins pointed and jutting; Private Breger and his friends have soft and rounded chins, while sergeants' chins are between the two extremes.

The differences in approach between little men in the American army and Japanese soldiers, rigorously trained and taught to believe implicitly in their duty to fight and die for Japan is most striking, and is echoed in the visual diet available to the two armies and indeed the two nations. Editorial cartoons on the European or American model had appeared in Japan at the end of the nineteenth century; there was even for a time a Japanese *Punch*. The older indigenous tradition of visual narrative in Japan also continued, but was fictional rather than commenting on events; that was left to the newspapers. However, during the 1930s, the freedom of the press to comment was much

(**left**) *Gordon Minhinnick set out to amuse in this strip,
which appeared in the* New Zealand Herald, *but was also
syndicated. Minhinnick was the main cartoonist for the
paper from 1930, and became the doyen of the country's
cartoonists, being knighted in 1976, as Low had been in
1965.*

*This anti-British drawing refers to the war in Burma. Such
pictures would be used by Japanese storytellers, impressing
local people with the idea of Britain's inferiority. The
tradition of storytelling was revived in Japan immediately
after the war, when 10,000 people are said to have used it
as a way of making a living.*

ROOSEVELT

He appeared on the cover of Manga, *drawn by the
magazine's editor Kondo Hidezo. Kondo was a leading
cartoonist who had helped found an independent cartoonist
organization in 1932, but he turned to propaganda in
1939, and was sent as a cartoonist to Borneo during the
war. Anti-American images included targets in schools,
which pupils could practise attacking, and the American
flag was painted on pavements so that it could be walked
over. Roosevelt, however, was in the company of Churchill
and Stalin as being on a* Manga *cover portrayed with fangs.
Roosevelt's death was welcomed in a national newspaper as
Heaven's punishment.*

curtailed. The war with China gave militarism a decisive hold and opposition was crushed. An unpopular view expressed by a cartoonist could result in jail and torture. One unlucky cartoonist who suffered such treatment in 1933 left Japan and went to live in the United States. During the war he created a cartoon strip, *Unganaizo* (the unlucky soldier), which appeared in *Rakhasen Nyusu* (Parachute News), a propaganda vehicle intended to undermine Japanese army morale.

The tenor of Japanese cartoons in the newspapers was strongly nationalistic. There was also *Manga*, a cartoon magazine which reproduced drawings by members of a group of patriotic cartoonists called *Shin Mangaha Shudan*. This had been formed by the merging of other groups, which the authorities had played off against each other. The sort of images used in *Manga* were as denigratory as any during the war, including a remarkable caricature of Roosevelt with fangs, by Kondo, the magazine's editor.

Adventure cartoon strips had been popular in the years before the war, some of them with a sub-text of Japanese superiority to other peoples, though there were some strips imported from America. A favourite Japanese strip was about a dog, *Nora-Kuro* (Black Stray); this series ran from 1931 to 1941, had a military setting and was often imperialistic in tone. The author was Tagawa Suiho.

The propagandist character of the press was not approved by everyone; for example, Yamamoto, architect of the attack on Pearl Harbor,

AUSTRALIA SCREAMS

This is an example of psychological warfare to discourage Australian troops. It was some way off target, just like an attempt to exploit differences between the Scots and the English troops in Hong Kong in 1941. Japanese cartoonists were able to draw in a Western style, but after the war found initial difficulty in returning to Japanese imagery.

'Charge!'

wrote privately: 'This war will give us much trouble in the future. The fact that we have had a small success at Pearl Harbor is nothing. The fact that we have succeeded so easily has pleased people. Personally I do not think it is a good thing to whip up propaganda to encourage the nation. People should think things over and realize how serious the situation is.' Serious reflection was not the temper of Japanese public opinion, fed by military success and fortified by a code of obedience. Nor was there any official intimation that anything might go wrong until the loss of Saipan in 1944, which, unlike previous areas of conflict, was within radio range of Japan.

This is a panel by Tagawa from the comic strip Nora Kuro *(Black Stray), which achieved considerable popularity in the 1930s and ran until 1941. The storyline was about a dog who joined the army, rising in rank to captain; in this panel he is a lieutenant leading his troops into battle. The dogs fought other animal armies. The strip's militarist tone was acceptable in a climate of opinion when Japanese expansion in China was felt to be justified.*

Chapter 5

HOME FRONTS

The Second World War copied the First in involving whole nations, not just armies and navies, as in previous centuries. The ultimate victory of the Allied nations over the Axis powers depended on manpower and on superiority of armaments and manufacturing capacity, a war of resources. Military skill and the professionalism of the German army could only achieve temporary success. Japan did not have the resources to continue a long war, however determined her military leaders and however fiercely her soldiers fought.

This involvement of whole nations in both wars spread the geography of war to industrial cities, and to civilians as targets. The war front was not only opposite enemy lines, but also in the home. The war for civilians meant the bombing of major cities, both as industrial targets and in deliberate attempts to destroy morale. Britain, Germany, Japan and Russia all suffered severely, while in other countries Rotterdam, Antwerp and Warsaw were prominent casualties. The issue of strategic bombing has been a subject of much dispute by historians, and was a controversial topic during the war. It was also an important subject for cartoonists.

A number of responses to bombing may be distinguished. One was stoicism. The most anthologized British example of stoicism is perhaps a cartoon by Strube of the *Daily Express*; the air raid is over and a keen amateur

'Yes, quite blitzy tonight.'

The air raids were a fruitful source of ideas for cartoonists, who enjoyed making light of the war, as Lee does in this cartoon from the Evening News. *American and other international syndication of cartoons broadcast British attitudes to the raids, which were also sympathetically reported by journalists working in Britain.*

AFTER THE RAID
'Is it all right now, Henry?'
'Yes, not even scratched.'

Sidney Strube's calm picture appeared in the Daily Express *in 1940. He was the paper's cartoonist for 36 years from 1910. During the Blitz Strube's little man became an air-raid warden; he discarded his old-fashioned garb for more practical clothes, while we can assume that his wife was knitting for war work. The cartoonist's well-earned respect from his readers came from his ability to express feelings which thousands had in common, in this case a stoic sense of humour at the discomforts of the war.*

gardener has emerged from his shelter to check on a giant marrow, which he tells his wife is untouched by the bombs. This solid citizen with an understanding of the things in life that really matter is a well-loved cartoon personality, who achieved fame in the years after the First World War as the 'Little Man'. The urban figure in a bowler hat and rather old-fashioned clothes personified a target for injustice of all sorts; the 'Little Man' is the over-burdened taxpayer, the sufferer from national and local bureaucracies, the plain voter who wants to be told about straightforward issues. In war it was natural for Strube to extend the roll-call of his oppressors from home to abroad.

British cartoonists also had a steady line in slogans like 'Business as Usual'. An official war artist saw the slogan on a wall in a bombed area of London saying 'We can take it': this was a spirit of defiance echoed in many gag cartoons.

Cartoons in the British newspapers were seen by an increasing number of people, as circulation figures went up from ten million in 1937 to fifteen and a half million in 1947. It was reported in the latter year that only seven newspapers out of 225 failed to make a profit. The press was in a healthy financial state during the war, and indeed the boom continued until 1950. One of the attractions of papers in one of the leading newspaper groups, the Beaverbrook Press, was undoubtedly the work of the cartoonists, Strube on the *Daily Express* and Low on the *Evening Standard*. Their work was financially well rewarded. When it became known that Strube had been offered £10,000 a year by a rival paper, his salary was immediately increased to that amount. Low certainly earned his salary; his independence of editorial policy

Schlacht im Atlantik

Zeichnung: Kraft (Interpred)

„Was sehn Sie durchs Glas, Admiral?"
„Einige unserer Schiffe treiben auf dem Wasser, einige sinken,
    einige fliegen in die Luft."
„Well, schreiben Sie: Die Wendigkeit unserer Kriegsmittel ist
    bereits dreidimensional."

**BATTLE IN
THE ATLANTIC**
'What do you see through
the glasses, Admiral?'
'A few of our ships are
proceeding on the water,
a few are sinking, and a
few are flying through the
air.'
'Well, write! The
manoeuvrability of our
war machinery is already
three dimensional.'

*This cartoon by Kraft
appeared in* Völkischer
Beobachter.

was an added asset, for it generated publicity when readers wrote in to complain. The other main groups also had assets in cartoonists, not least the strip-cartoon *Jane* in the *Daily Mirror*.

The pattern of press organization in Britain was one of rivalry, without the syndication which was a feature of the American press. In the thirties there had been strenuous circulation wars, as papers tried to buy readers by presents and gimmicks for subscribers; this competition had taken both the *Daily Express* and the *Daily Herald* over the two million mark. Of the press barons, Beaverbrook was the most remarkable, often intervening in his papers' work. An editor who worked for him on the *Daily Express* commented that 'leading articles, feature ideas,

news stories, gossip paragraphs, criticism and praise flooded over the telephone' from him 'hour by hour'.

There was some tension between the press and politicians, not helped by the role of the Ministry of Information being enfeebled by a need to get agreement from the armed services for the release of news. Such tension did not spill over into the censorship of cartoons, but then that was of a piece with the acceptance by the press of the policy lines adopted by the government. Ideas were dropped well before they might have reached the point of being censored. This consensus did not prevent cartoonists having some fun at the expense of the ministries, bureaucracy and restrictions.

**BATTLE OF
THE ATLANTIC**

Stephen devised a simple line formula for the faces of Churchill and Roosevelt, employed in this unrealistically cheerful image of the Allied situation in the Atlantic war.

Some cartoons arose directly out of the ministries' work, for example in popularizing campaigns for purposes such as 'The Battle for Fuel' or 'Eat More Potatoes'. The Minister for Food was Lord Woolton. He had the sunny idea of asking advice from Walt Disney, who suggested cartoon characters to further the 'Dig for Victory' policy; Dr Carrot and Potato Pete duly appeared in poster campaigns. One of the success stories of publicity was the invention of a character for dissuading people from unnecessary purchases. The Squander Bug was the invention of Philip Boydell, and was taken up by cartoonists with enthusiasm. The unmistakeable creature, covered with swastikas, cackled his way with glee through the shops, impoverishing housewives and helping the enemy by wasting resources.

The art of caption writing was in firm demand for publicity. A fuel economy label, for example, had 'Switched-on switches and turned on taps/Make happy Huns and joyful Japs'; a transport ministry campaign featured a surreal image of a scene at a bus stop, 'Elephants are out of place in a rush hour queue/So Are Shoppers'; and a double-decker bus complains, 'Yes, doctor, it's my feet/Rubber is a munition of war/take great care of your tyres.'

Good humour was also the tone of cartoon contributions to some of the other publications cherished by wartime readers. *Lilliput* was a cheerful publication, with good stories and amusing illustrations, started by Stephan Lorant, also responsible for a major success of the war, *Picture Post*. The Czech cartoonist Walter Trier was the man who drew the covers for *Lilliput* as well as some pointed anti-Nazi material in the magazine. *Blighty*, a light-

'He complained that his horse dated him so.'

This light-hearted joke by Neb, pocket cartoonist for the Daily Mail, *can also be a reminder of the transformation of British cavalry into tank regiments. Horses are rare in Second World War cartoons, having lost their military importance and even their symbolic significance as rulers' mounts (though both Mussolini and Hirohito had ceremonial white horses).*

(**right**) *This* Lilliput *cover by Walter Trier is typical of his consistent level of blithe invention for a long series of covers. He had a formula: 'The couple was the embodiment of something eternally amusing – youth, love – and the little Scotch terrier out of regard for the English love of animals, and as a memento to Zottle and Maggy, my companions for many years. I refused from the outset to keep to a definite type of couple. Sometimes they are young, sometimes older, sometimes naturalistic and sometimes stylized, in all possible costumes of all sorts of periods, not even always of flesh and blood, but as chopped trees or fruit or often as toys.'*

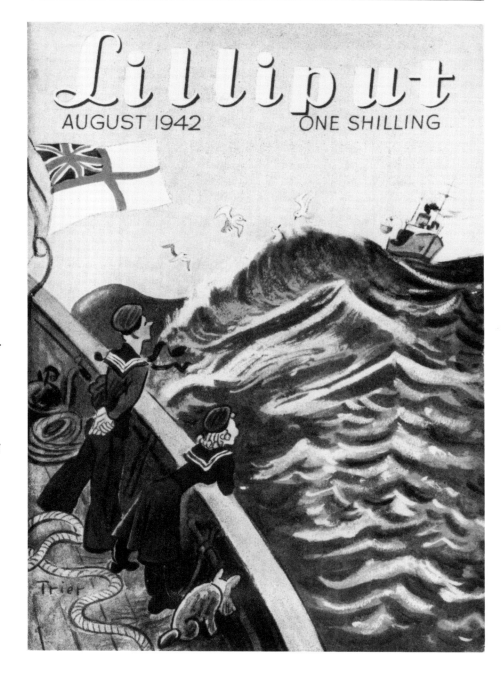

'Thaird floor! No crockery, no hardware,
no toys, and precious little baby linen.'

(**left**) *Osbert Lancaster drew his pocket cartoon for the* Daily Express, *his best-known characters being a social set of well-born cocktail-party-goers. During the war he served in the Foreign Office, and in this cartoon he picks on London office and shop life which he saw around him.*

(**right**) *Helen Hokinson was a gifted* New Yorker *artist, with a sharp eye for the foibles of clubwomen, nicknamed the Hokinson Girls; she used gags from* New Yorker *staff writers. The resulting productions may be said to have answered an early description of the magazine's character:* 'The New Yorker *will be what is commonly called sophisticated, in that it will assume a reasonable degree of enlightenment on the part of its readers.' Those readers during the war included the US armed forces, for whom a miniature lightweight edition was produced.*

hearted magazine both for the services and the home market, made a feature of cartoons laced with sexual innuendo.

Humour had a star role in British cartoons for the home front. A useful guide for the policy-makers was an early study of popular sentiment made by an independent organization called Mass Observation, which made impressionistic reports of what people felt about war issues. The man in the street, it was said, did not like being overdosed with patriotic sentiment. As a result poster policy was altered by the govern-ment. One man with his finger firmly on the public pulse was undoubtedly Kenneth Bird, the art editor of *Punch* who specialized in stick-figure cartoons with witty captions. His name as a cartoonist was Fougasse, and he was much in demand; he generously did official posters free of charge.

Fougasse commented lucidly and thoughtfully on informational posters. He argued that they had to overcome three main obstacles: 'firstly, a general aversion to reading a notice of any sort; secondly, a general disinclination to believe that any notice, even if read, can possibly be addressed to oneself; thirdly, a general unwilling-

'Miss Whitehead will tell us how to amuse sailors.'

ness, even so, to remember the message long enough to do anything about it.' Further, 'A poster cannot prove anything...if it tries to prove too much, or to protest too much, it will automatically defeat its own object.' Fougasse used humour to good effect in his work, asserting that 'The function of humour is essentially corrective: it is a corrective, for instance, of incongruity and of faulty proportion.' It is in this sense that Fougasse transformed the overbearing figures of Hitler and Goering into comic characters, sitting in a bus eavesdropping on a housewives' conversation.

Humour of the gentler sort has been a mainstay of British twentieth-century cartooning, and the war gave plenty of opportunity for its exercise. *Punch* had several other brilliant practitioners. Pont's special preserve was the recognizably self-assured upper and middle classes in a state of unruffled calm. An anthology of his cartoons was published in 1940 with the suitable title *The British Carry On*. A finely drawn ink line added to the effect of Pont's well-aimed satire of people and their surroundings.

It was to be expected of *Punch* that the professional and middle classes, the bulk of the paper's readership, would feature largely in its

'You'd think with less food there would be fewer dishes.'

This heartfelt grumble by Norman Fallon is in the category of married couple jokes, which fuelled a successful group of strip cartoons such as Blondie, *as well as gag cartoons. This one is from* Collier's Weekly.

The affluent apartment described by Robert Day for his New Yorker audience is a good backdrop for a joke about war shortages. Robert Day contributed as a freelancer to a variety of journals, including the Saturday Evening Post, Look, and even Punch. British and American humour had much in common at this level. At the New Yorker there were no 'cartoons', only drawings by artists; at Punch the influence of Fougasse as art editor was towards publishing fewer drawings with long dialogue captions, the standard form in the nineteenth century which had the nickname of a 'three act play'.

'One lump or none?'

This neat visual quip about food shortages in the United States by Ving Fuller appeared in Collier's Weekly. *Hundreds of panel cartoons were drawn for daily and weekly papers, and also trade papers, to which some cartoonists specialized in sending their work.*

pages. Sillince drew in a broad pencil line for his tweed-costumed lady out walking in the country, dispassionately observing birds' nests and a machine-gun nest. A sharp eye for clothes can be found in the work of Anton, the *nom de plume* of a lady and her brother, who pinpointed a sort of shady businessman, not necessarily quite on the right side of the law, for whom the new name of 'spiv' was invented.

Exponents of urban humour included Lee and David Langdon. Giles was a social satirist who began a long reign; he moved easily from major political subjects to entertaining street characters, instantly recognizable and remembered. Less extensive in scope but sharply observed were the pocket cartoons of Osbert Lancaster in the *Daily Express*, who parodied and pilloried a social set for whose absurdities he evidently could not help feeling affection.

Some foreigners have thought that the British are overconfident about their possession of a sense of humour, which did not perhaps play too important a part along the road to victory. It must nevertheless have been a useful safety valve in pictorial art as well as in other ways, to judge, for example, by the considerable popularity of a programme like Tommy Handley's ITMA (It's That Man Again) on radio. There was no comparable programme in German broadcasting, which was dedicated to a more strenuous form of building and maintaining morale. The German propaganda ministry's information-gathering system was especially thorough, and the radio was a major means of communication, followed, however, by the meticulously planned mass meetings of which Goebbels was a complete master. Cartoons were low in a scale of priority within such a scheme.

'It's a new species they've found in the minefields.'

Shortages of food produced verbal and visual jokes, of which this surrealistic combination of fish and mine is a pleasant example by Neb. The British wartime table included the doubtful delicacies of whale meat and the curiously named snoek, as well as carrot jam and a meatless Woolton pie, named for the Minister of Food.

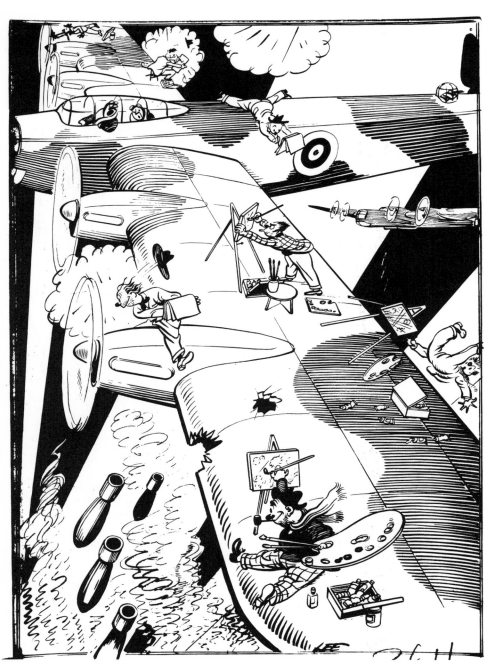

'First it was reporters, and now it's official artists.'

Lee's cartoon in the Evening News *recalls the British scheme of patronage which created an artistic record of the war in more than 5500 paintings, watercolours, drawings and other works of art. The war was not easy to record; air battles were at high speed, and there were limits to depicting the menace of bombing; tank battles, and, even more, sea battles were fought at long range.*

'Charlie says not to forget he wants his war medals back by ten o'clock.'

This cartoon is from Private Breger in Britain, *an anthology published in 1944. Breger was a notable writer of slogans – he suggested 'Our Wurst is the Best' for his father's Chicago sausage factory; no surprise, then, to learn that he invented the character of GI Joe as a successor to Private Breger; the initials stood for Government Issue. The tag was a wildfire success, and American soldiers everywhere became GIs.*

'The Squander Bug.'

(left) *Phillip Boydell's cartoon character was versatile. Originally intended to help the British National Savings campaigns, the bug was extensively used by cartoonists, Vicky, Zec, Giles and Low among them; it was given a place in Madame Tussauds' waxworks with other war enemies such as Hitler. Boydell was responding with humour to a moment when people were 'getting high wages for hard work and producing little or nothing to spend it on'. The Squander Bug was also a riposte to endless government publicity about what not to do: 'Don't waste fuel! Don't show a light!' The Squander Bug was positive: 'Go on, be an idiot! Buy it! and waste your money!'*

'You never know who's listening.'

(top, right) *This poster by Fougasse was one of a series of eight, 'Careless Talk costs Lives', in the style of his* Punch *cartoons. Fougasse became art editor of* Punch *in 1934, and continued until he took the job of editor in 1949.*

(bottom, right) *A fuel economy label by Fougasse.*

You never know who's listening!

CARELESS TALK COSTS LIVES

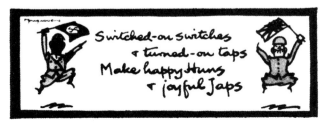

Switched-on switches & turned-on taps Make happy Huns & joyful Japs

In Germany fears of bombing were more difficult to discount with humour, since the force of Nazi propaganda had been towards asserting the supremacy of the Aryan race, and to be dismissive of Britain; the logical development of this attitude was to treat bombing with disdain and contempt. But, after Stalingrad, Goebbels changed the general tenor of his propaganda to arguing that sacrifices would be needed for the fulfilment of Germany's destiny. In any case, the facts of heavy bombing made nonsense of claims for the power, to say nothing of the invincibility of the Luftwaffe.

Another tactic was to respond to bombing with vows of vengeance. Hitler's injured pride at the enemy bombing of German cities found some outlet in the plans for secret weapons, the rocket bombs. Goebbels persuaded him to name these with the initial for the word in German for retribution, *Vergeltung*, the first being called VI to imply a sequence of ever-increasing deadly weapons. In fact, by the time the rockets were employed, the Propaganda Ministry had decided to play down the theme of retribution as being unlikely to be an adequate reinforcement of morale.

In another sphere of morale, Germany was more successful; there was no slackening of effort in the factories, and the extent of production of armaments and other goods was maintained to a degree far beyond what was believed by the advocates of strategic bombing as a means of ending the war. The positive attitude of pride in Germany and the country's destiny, promoted by propaganda and reinforced by cartoons, paid off in this respect.

The other aspect of the home front to be considered is the matter of supplies. Germany's

**SHUTTING OUT
THE SUN**

*Wyndham Robinson's
cartoon for the* Star *has
a gloomy theme with its
symbolism of the destruction
of ships by submarine
warfare. A generalized
cartoon of this sort was
one of the ways of drawing
attention to the war at sea,
of which details were
frequently scarce. Robinson
had formerly been
cartoonist for the* Morning
Post; *he served in Burma
during the war.*

initial advantage of military successes in 1939 and 1940 was to provide a substantial source of goods from the whole of western Europe. An early cartoon by Partridge alleged hardship in Germany, but this was far from the mark, and, in fact, an inaccurate historical parallel from the First World War when the British blockade of Germany had been seriously damaging. The German army and the nation were in a position to drain resources from their occupied territories. It was only in the later stages of the war that hardship began to be felt, and that hardship fell much heavier on other countries than on Germany.

Germany was on the attack in the question of supplies, since the German navy was able to

'The price of petrol has been increased by one penny. "Official".'

Zec's cartoon appeared in the Daily Mirror, *and was intended to make readers reflect on the importance of economizing on fuel, which reached Britain by sea at a high cost in seamen's lives. The cartoon caused a storm, and was discussed in the Houses of Parliament. Ironically, the caption was not Zec's own; it had been thought up by one of his colleagues to give the picture more impact.*

threaten the merchant shipping which brought essentials to the British Isles. Only occasionally did convoys and submarine attacks feature in editorial cartoons, although the threat to Britain was used in Germany, and British sinkings of U-Boats occur in British papers. The war at sea is not a prominent part of cartooning in the war; part of the reason is the difficulty of isolating events which could be portrayed as decisive, unlike the capture of a city like Rome, or the drama of an invasion.

One of the few controversial British cartoons of the war was drawn by Zec of the *Daily Mirror*. It was called 'The Price of Petrol', and was intended to highlight the risks taken by sailors bringing supplies to Britain; a seaman is seen dead on a raft. Churchill wrongly interpreted the cartoon as a criticism of the government's conduct of the war. The newspaper only just escaped being banned.

Chapter 6
THE MEDITERRANEAN

The war in the Mediterranean and North Africa was the outcome of European imperialism, through which North Africa had been divided into French rule in the west (Morocco, Algeria and Tunisia), Italian rule in the centre (Libya) and the far east (Ethiopia), while the British held sway, if not theoretically power, in Egypt. Italian armies in Libya numbered 200,000 men, and in Ethiopia a further 215,000.

In August, 1940, a significant British force, including a third of all available tanks, was sent to Egypt. This disposition made a desert war inevitable. General O'Connor was responsible for an attack on Libya, which succeeded in taking 130,000 Italian prisoners, at the cost of 438 Australian and British dead; by February, 1941, eastern Libya was in British hands.

Events moved swiftly in 1941. Italy had declared war on Greece, but the campaign had been slow to succeed. Hitler decided to aid his ally. German troops in April invaded Yugoslavia where a patriotic opposition to Germany was

CASABLANCA

Edgar, a South American cartoonist, shows France as a bride for Hitler eloping instead with Roosevelt. The swastika as a distorted cross is carried by Laval as a priest ready to celebrate Hitler's marriage, and is a decoration for Pétain.

THE WALK-OVER WAR

Sidney Strube in the Daily Express *here makes fun of Mussolini's military ambitions, strengthening his ridicule by pidgin Italian-English. Special languages were a frequent feature of strip cartoons, where text and image work together to make the narrative go forward. Editorial cartoons rely more on images.*

crushed; the surrender was signed on 17 April. Greece was invaded by the German army, and to support the Greeks a British force was sent from North Africa. The Greek army was almost immediately defeated, and few British troops were in action. 40,000 British troops and 10,000 Greeks were evacuated, including the King and his government. The majority of the British troops went to Crete. This was not a haven. German paratroops were landed on 20 May, 1941, and Crete was captured; 13,000 British and Commonwealth troops were taken prisoner.

Meanwhile, in Ethiopia British troops from Egypt and Kenya, together with Abyssinians raised in revolt by the former Emperor, attacked the Italian army. On 6 April, 1941, the capital, Addis Ababa, was taken. The main body of the Italian army surrendered on 20 May.

Loss of his troops to the Greek campaign had prevented O'Connor from proceeding to western Libya to take Tripoli. The city was reinforced from Germany by a panzer division, later made into the Afrika Korps. A swift raid by Rommel, the new commander, took British forces by surprise, and by 11 April, 1941, the British gains were all lost, except Tobruk, and O'Connor had been captured.

Rommel captured Tobruk in June, 1942, taking almost the whole garrison of 35,000 as prisoners, and gaining important fuel, vehicles and supplies. It was a triumph for him and a disaster for the British Eighth Army whose general was dismissed. Montgomery became

Die serbische Marionette

SERBIAN PUPPETRY
'Wait a moment, Mr Churchill.'

The cartoon appears in a book with quotations from Churchill's speeches, ironically illustrated. The artist was a notorious figure in Nazi cultural life. Mjölnir was responsible for anti-Semitic images in Die Angriff from the beginning of the party's rise to power; he held a powerful administrative position in the Reich Chamber of Culture, and was named as professor. Mjölnir was a prolific poster designer. At the end of the war he committed suicide.

the new commander of the Eighth Army. In October, 1942, Montgomery won a decisive victory at El Alamein, and Rommel's army was in retreat.

Montgomery arrived in North Africa determined to improve the morale of his army, whose officers and men he believed to have been disheartened by the desert campaign. He was outstandingly successful in achieving this aim and became a hero in Britain as well as in Egypt. His flair for personal publicity was a valuable asset. His adversary, Rommel, had the luck to be commanding tanks in a terrain where his gifts showed to advantage. He earned the admiring nickname of the Desert Fox. Montgomery put up a reproduction of a portrait of him in one of his campaign caravans and refused to be intimidated. If there was to be a war of minds, he would win that as well as military battles. He played up his own character as decisive and determined, and visited troops in all parts of his command. He impressed them. Standing on a jeep, a single soldier surrounded by soldiers, he was also a memorable figure in cinema newsreels. For the rest of the war he was the military leader who carried popular conviction. He was an easily identifiable personality for cartoonists, especially with two cap-badges on his beret. He was a welcome new figure for the editorial pages of *Punch* and the newspapers.

Another means of building morale in the army was through cartoon characters with whom soldiers could identify. Two such personalities were created by a Welsh Guards officer, W. J. Jones, known by his pen name of Jon. The 'Two Types' appeared in North Africa and accompanied the Eighth Army to Italy. They became cherished symbols of the army's determination.

'You see, we put the fifth one away for the duration.'

Joss was cartoonist for the Star, *a job he had reached after a wandering youth in Europe and South America (he was a cartoonist in Rio de Janiero at 19). During his war service as a gunner, he drew under the name of Denim. In this cartoon he asserts that Greece had no citizens favourable to the Italo-German invasion. The term 'fifth-column' is attributed to a Fascist general in the Spanish Civil War. He said that his four columns of troops advancing on Madrid were complemented by a fifth column of supporters in the capital. Hemingway used the phrase for the title of a play.*

The appeal of the 'Two Types' owes much to the style of the cartoonist, whose breezy decisive line echoes the devil-may-care approach of his characters. The introduction to one of the published anthologies of the cartoons explains how they appealed in more than one way:

The Fair Type and the Dark Type are thin figures rather than sharply characterized each in his own right. The more aggressive Dark Type does most of the shouting, while the Fair Type has a 'battered beret and look of Popeye'd astonishment at a world packed with surprises'. All the same, the captions often express the combined attitude of the two of them, who, for all their deceptively fatuous appearance are characters of violence and action. Their attitude to the world and everyone in it is 'Hit or miss'. Either you like us or you hate us. We don't worry a damn either way.

The two debonair officers are partners in their adventures, which suitably include the everyday difficulties of army life; mechanical troubles with transport, or running out of petrol, are examples of such themes. Their uniforms are personal, as unorthodox as Montgomery's cap-badges, and they employ the sardonic wit of

'Look, darling, a British lion!'

This unexpected twist to the tail of British pride appeared in Vox. *Numbers of* Vox *used quotations from the Allied press, making fun of the texts with cartoons; captions are in three languages.*

'We'll soon be digging in at Shepheard's.'

Jon (W.J. Jones) here draws with characteristic bravura his 'Two Types', looking forward to reaching a famous Cairo hotel. His editor recorded that Jon had 'worked with me and a gang of restless soldiers (all newspaper professionals in peacetime) who produced instant daily papers for the British services in a dozen or more cities stretching from Algiers to Klagenfurt in Austria.'

"We'll soon be digging in at Shepheard's"

seasoned veterans; the comment about a new arrival, impeccably turned out, is a grunt – 'Must be a soldier'. American troops in North Africa and Italy were not all immaculately uniformed, though it is difficult to believe there were many to match the decrepit and unsavoury appearances of Bill Mauldin's 'Willie and Joe'. Mauldin's career as a cartoonist was meteoric. He joined the army as a teenager and, though his first cartoons were refused by *Yank*, they soon got acceptance on the 45th Division paper, and he established a special position for himself. His characters were safety valves for troops living and fighting in depressing conditions, but all the same making a job of it.

Mauldin was an army private when, under fire, he was awarded a Purple Heart. This adds a piquant footnote for the reader of his picture of a soldier refusing a medal in favour of aspirin.

Mauldin is one of the few cartoonists of the war to have written an autobiography, which contains some hilarious stories and plentiful evidence of his enterprise, not least in finding means to print service magazines with his cartoons in them. His personal popularity was great, especially among the many young soldiers of his own age, and his usefulness was recognized by his being given his own jeep. General Patton was less easy to impress. One of the funniest episodes in Mauldin's book is the account of his

**LITTLE KNOWN UNITS OF THE WESTERN DESERT.
NO 791 MISINFORMATION POST**

being summoned to meet the General, who was sure the cartoons were bad for military discipline. Mauldin survived the encounter.

He had a firm grasp of his aims and his audience. He did not mind irritating the brass or the staff behind the lines so long as he appealed to the infantryman at the front. He was deliberately partisan.

I'm concerned that the infantry is the group in the army which gives more and gets less than anybody else. I draw pictures for and about dogfaces because I know what their life is like, and I understand their gripes.

Brian Robb described his series of cartoons as having been 'conceived at dinner in the Mess of a S B P & M Coy. (Sign Board Painting and Maintenance Company) . . . as the series developed and people looked upon them, they began to appreciate the full extent of the results achieved by Road Obstruction Companies, Misinformation Posts, and other industrious groups of Britishers who patiently and unobtrusively carried out their duties in various parts of the desert.'

This is one of the famous American cartoons of the war by Bill Mauldin. Mauldin's strong partisanship for the infantry is here well expressed by a stoic indifference to honours.

'Just gimme th'aspirin, I already got a Purple Heart.'

Mauldin drew this cartoon for a British services newspaper. It touched a sore point for the British who were surprised at the lavish resources of the American army, and the way in which equipment was left unreclaimed after a battle.

'You blokes leave an awfully messy battlefield.'

They don't get fancy pay, they know their food is the worst in the army because you can't whip up lemon pies or even hot soup at the front, and they know how much of the burden they bear.

He also accepted his limitations: 'I haven't tried to picture this war in a big, broad-minded way.

I'm not old enough to understand what it's all about, and I'm not experienced enough to judge its failures and successes. My reactions are those of a young guy who has been exposed to some of it, and I try to put those reactions in my drawings. Since I'm a cartoonist, maybe I can be funny after the war, but nobody who has seen

Mauldin's cartoon is one more shot in a never-ending battle between the men at the front and their officers, especially in headquarters staff behind the lines.

'Them buttons wuz shot off when I took this town, sir.'

this war can be cute about it while it's going on.'

Finally he created characters who were rough diamonds: 'True, Joe and Willie don't look much like the cream of young American manhood who was sent overseas in the infantry. Neither of them is boyish, although neither is aged. Joe is in his early twenties and Willie is in his early thirties — pretty average age for the infantry...their expressions are those of infantry soldiers who have been in the war for a couple of years.' And then again, 'Willie and Joe aren't at all clever. They aren't even good cartoon characters, because they have similar features which are distinguishable only by their different

'We'll march together. (Mussolini)'

The Australian cartoonist Clive Uptton comments on the two dictators in partnership against Greece. Hitler reluctantly came to the help of his ally, who had given no warning of his attack on Greece. This cartoon is reproduced in a wartime book which starts: 'To the Greek soldier who, in the mountains of Albania, defeated Fascist Italy on a piece of bread and a handful of black olives, this book is proudly dedicated.'

noses. Willie has a big nose and Joe has a little one. The bags under their eyes and the dirt in their ears is so similar that few people know which is Willie and which is Joe.'

Their fellow soldiers were among those who joined Eisenhower's joint American and British force to invade North-West Africa in November and December, 1942. The French authorities signed an armistice in December. Since De Gaulle was unacceptable to the local French authorities, Giraud was made French High Commissioner.

In March Rommel was in a bad position, since the Allied forces had been strongly reinforced, and Rommel's attack against them failed. He soon afterwards gave up his command. British troops entered Tunis on 7 May, 1943.

The way was clear for an invasion of Sicily, which was undertaken on 10 July. By 16 August American troops under Patton and British troops under Montgomery had taken the island. Italy became divided. The King dismissed Mussolini. The new Prime Minister, Badoglio, made peace for Italy in September. But the Germans were ready to fight on and disarmed the Italian troops. Italy declared war on Germany in October. The complicated position was that the Italian government had little effective power, whereas the Germans had an army in the field. Further, the Italian resistance was as much opposed to the monarchy as to the Germans.

Italy's surrender had removed from the cartoon war a valued target for Allied cartoonists. Hitler and Mussolini were a cartoon comedy turn as familiar as Bud Abbott and Lou Costello in film. The variety of costumes and situations was enormous. In the 1930s Low had run a

THE CRANES
OF IBYCUS

The failure of British promises was a fruitful source of German cartooning at the beginning of the war when Poland, Czechoslovakia, Finland and Norway had not received effective help. The imagery is a classical story in modern dress. The Greek poet Ibycus was murdered near Corinth, but before he died he called to a flock of cranes to avenge him. This story from Greece in the sixth century BC was the theme of a poem by Schiller.

Zeichnung: Bogner

Die Kraniche des Ibykus...

(left) *David Langdon was a prolific cartoonist in the war, contributing to* Punch, *but also drawing cartoons for service papers as a serving member of the RAF. Scarcity of reading matter made this appeal one of many. The drawing was done for the inside cover of a collection of drawings, 'All buttoned up!'*

'Pass this little book on when you've had it . . .'

(below) *A cartoon by Virgil Partch in* Collier's Weekly. *Partch was a freelance gag cartoonist, who had worked for a time in the Disney studios. His hallmark was a witty literal-mindedness, which resulted in such a picture as someone being 'dug up' for a party.*

"There's the typical censor for you"

cartoon strip about two dictators, 'Hit and Muss'. During the war cartoonists used two alternative strategies: the pair were presented as equals, say on a see-saw, on a tandem bicycle or sitting on a park bench; on the other hand they could be depicted in conflict, quarrelling, with, say, one in a child's role to the other's parent. Italy's entry into the war, for example, was shown as Hitler the mother telling the child Mussolini that it was time for his bath – of blood. Hitler on his own was not so good to draw; indeed Low even complained about his uninteresting facial features, and Partridge much preferred Mussolini's strong face.

Mussolini was a helpfully bombastic dictator, for whom an imperial toga was appropriate clothing. In Italy this sort of allusion was even made seriously, to go with the emblems of fasces from which Fascism took its name. Cartoonists attacking Fascism mostly preferred the swastika as a hate symbol, partly for its associations as an apparently deformed cross. The Italian press was not as tightly controlled as the German, but then in Italy, despite the length of Mussolini's reign, there was a greater diversity of political opinion. One could deduce from Italian graphic material that the conquest of Abyssinia had been a romantic adventure; certainly not, like Germany's domination of Europe, a call of destiny.

Mussolini was imprisoned by the Italian government, but was rescued by the Germans and established as the leader of a Fascist Social Republic, run by German administrators. The end of his story came a year later when he was killed by Italian partisans at Dongo near Lake Como, having tried to escape to Germany. His importance in politics had ceased, but his fate

SPLITTING THE SWAG
'What are you grumbling for, Benito? You've got what you asked for, haven't you?'

Partridge's cartoon was inspired by an official American estimate of loot taken from occupied Europe. It appeared in Punch *in May, 1943.*

JM BAUCHE DES BÄREN

IN THE STOMACH OF THE BEAR

Gulbransson's intelligent line is here used to analyze the situation at the conference of Teheran, where he considers that Stalin will have his way.

was a topic for moralizing cartoons, some of which were vindictive. His imperialistic pride as *Il Duce* received particular attention. Throughout his life self-identification with the Roman empire had given cartoonists their opportunities for a dramatic scenario; his death confirmed that the play was ended.

The Italian campaign progressed slowly in 1944 as the Germans established strong lines of defence. Rome was blocked by such a line; on the road to Rome, Monte Cassino was firmly defended. A landing was made at Anzio, thirty-three miles from Rome, to outflank the Cassino position. But it was not until 5 June, 1944, that the Allies entered Rome, which the Germans had by then abandoned for defensive lines beyond. That summer the Italian partisans were responsible for harassing the German troops in the north, and the mainly British army reached Ravenna. After a break in the winter, the advance was begun again in April, 1945. Turin, Milan and Genoa were captured, while Venice fell to the Italian partisans, and the picturesque leader of a private army, Popski. The Germans surrendered on 29 April, 1945.

Italy's complicated war history was echoed by an unusual pattern of newspaper and magazine publications. The Fascist régime exerted influence on the press, as on other facets of Italian life. In the 1930s propagandist material was produced for the Abyssinian war, including cartoons and postcards. Editorial cartoons were expected to favour the régime. Newspapers liked to include American cartoon strips, which enhanced sales even for so well established a paper as the *Corriere della Sera* of Milan. An adaption of an American favourite like Mickey Mouse was at home in Italy as Topolino. In the war there were some striking transformations; an example is the strip Mandrake – in 1941 in *L'Avventuroso* Nazi spies turned into Allies, the Gestapo became the American police, and Berlin became Washington.

Cartoon strips were popular in Italy, and had a considerable revival after the war, helped by the American presence during the Allied administration. But in the war zones between 1943 and 1945 production was small, even if in the German-backed northern state an attempt was made to keep things running normally. As in France, there were clandestine publications, though not on the same scale. The postwar revival of the Italian press was not as traumatic as in France, since Italy had never become a polarized nation. Independent views, rather, which there had always been, had a voice again.

THE FATES DECIDE

This major Punch *cartoon by Shepard about Teheran elevates the three Allied leaders into three fates, the sort of classical allusion to which* Punch *readers were assumed to be accustomed. The allusion is imprecise in interpretation, since the classical character of fates who cruelly decide without any concern for human consequences was hardly how the Allied leaders saw themselves, or were seen. E.H. Shepard's main gifts were as a book illustrator, although he was a competent cartoonist who filled the junior position on* Punch *to Bernard Partridge during the war. He is famous for his marvellously apt drawings for A.A. Milne's children's books, such as* Winnie the Pooh *and* The House at Pooh Corner.

Chapter 7

TOWARDS BERLIN

The shape of the war in the east changed decisively in 1944. The war of resources had been won by Russia, since the industry on which her armaments depended was out of range in Siberia and parts of Russia far away from the German front. The military war that was being waged skilfully by both sides had turned to the advantage of the Russians, with their greatly superior strength of numbers. The German army also suffered from the domination of Hitler as a strategist, since his military decisions often depended on considerations which had little to do with the military situation. For this reason the prominence of Hitler in cartoon warfare was fully justified. The reputations of the generals were seldom sufficient for them to be particularly noticed. The two exceptions in the hindsight of postwar history are Guderian and Rommel, both of whom established strong personal reputations.

The tentacles of an octopus are exploited by Vicky to portray Himmler's grip, through the Gestapo organization, on lives in Germany and occupied Europe. Efimov similarly portrayed Himmler as a spider. A spider is a common image in earlier centuries, also being a nickname for a spy-master or an exceptionally well-informed sovereign.

'Keeps rolling along.'

Stuart Preston, an Australian cartoonist, here demonstrates a natural confidence in the superior industrial and military resources of Russia. The punning use of a phrase from the popular song, 'Old Man River', together with the steamroller as a metaphor for unstoppable force shows how accessible varied sources are to a cartoonist. In 1943, the date of this cartoon, ultimate German victory seemed unlikely.

**THE NOVELTY OF
FASCIST TECHNOLOGY**

*The black humour used by
Kukryniksy approaches the
topic of the tragedies of
the German concentration
camps. Himmler was a
clearly identified target for
Russian cartoonists, and the
same team of artists
produced a remarkable and
savage portrait image of
him in a bloodstained
apron, one of a series of
such individual drawings.*

On the Russian side the personality of Zhukov was possibly the most impressive, and certainly the name with which foreign readers were most familiar.

In 1944 Leningrad was at last relieved, and it was honoured with the Order of Lenin. Probably the siege had been the cause of more than a million dead. Russian memories do not forget the courage of the inhabitants of Leningrad in conditions of danger and starvation. Russia regained her position on the Baltic, with the three states of Estonia, Latvia and Lithuania coming under Russian control. They never retrieved their independence, which had only lasted from 1920, when they had seceded from Russia, to 1940 when they had become incor-

THE GHETTO

The cartoon is from a book of drawings by Stanislaw Dobrzynski, mockingly called 'Sein Kampf' (His Struggle), in which Hitler is pilloried. His giant hand here hovers over man, woman and child in a ghetto for Jews.

porated into the Soviet Union.

German rule in the Baltic states had been disastrous for the Jewish population, of whom more than a quarter of a million were killed. Russian rule, though, was also feared and a further quarter of a million people emigrated to Germany or Sweden; it has been estimated that half a million people were deported to Russia in the period until 1949; about a quarter of those deported are said to have returned after Stalin's death in 1953. Such major historical movements are scarcely visible in cartoon history. A symbolic figure of *Exile* seems particularly inadequate for the task of representing massive shifts of population; and the scale of deaths cannot be clearly signified.

On 5 January, 1944, the Russian army crossed the pre-war frontier with Poland. In June this central advance in White Russia and Poland had resulted in major successes, with 350,000 German soldiers taken prisoner. Lvov was taken in July, and at the beginning of August the Russians were outside Warsaw, where they were opposed by three German armies.

The events that followed have been the subject of much bitter controversy, and, unlike the fate of the Baltic states, were prominently visible in cartoons outside Russia. The Polish government in exile in London had long hoped to take Warsaw with the forces of the Polish resistance before the Russians arrived; the commander in Poland intended that his Polish Home Army should 'come out in their full part as host to receive the entering Soviet armies'. The clear aim was to ensure that Polish independence would not be due to Russian conquest. The Home Army rose in Warsaw in August. The Russians gave little help, and, it is argued, were incapable of doing so; their lines

'Dogs! Would you live for ever?'

'Make up your mind, Bulgaria – you'll be better off in my bus.'

The tangled history of the Balkan states at the end of the war is recalled in this cartoon by Stephen, which shows the choice open to Bulgaria of joining with either Russia or Germany.

(left) *This notorious exclamation by Frederick of Prussia to his faltering troops is turned to a new use by Vicky. Frederick addresses his words to the Nazi leaders. Vicky was astute, and knew that comparisons of Hitler with Frederick the Great were stock in trade for German propaganda.*

of communication were undeniably very extended. The Warsaw uprising lasted for two months. The British and American air forces offered to fly in supplies to Warsaw, but the Russians did not provide landing facilities until the uprising was almost over. In the uprising 55,000 Poles were killed, and 350,000 were deported to Germany. The city was almost completely in ruins, and the Germans systematically

There was uncertainty about the situation in Yugoslavia, but Mihailovič was considered by British left-wing opinion to have sided with the German occupying forces. Hence the sardonic nature of this Vicky cartoon, in which Mihailovič is seated with German officers. Vicky was exceptionally alert to European politics, having worked in Berlin before being forced out and being employed, from 1939, by the News Chronicle. He made excellent use of a year the editor gave him to acclimatize himself to Britain, in 1950 worthily succeeding Low on the Evening Standard.

'Gentlemen, I've just received orders to start fighting you.'

(right) The Latin heading reads 'A name is an omen.'

destroyed what was left.

This was only part of the tragedy of Poland, for the loss of human life during the war was enormous — 5,800,000 dead. The Jewish people of Poland suffered most; of this figure they accounted for 3,200,000.

The Russian army did not capture Warsaw until January of the next year. Other Russian military advances in 1944 were impressive. There was a *coup d'état* against the pro-German government in Roumania; the country signed an armistice with Russia in September. In Bulgaria a declaration of war was followed by an armistice, enabling Russian forces to cross the country to Yugoslavia. In October Tito's Yugoslav partisans and Russian forces entered Belgrade, where Tito set up his independent Communist government. Russian forces occupied much of Hungary, although a German puppet government was in control of Budapest. But Russian forces had not reached Slovakia, where there was an uprising against the pro-German government; this was put down harshly.

The Russian campaign in 1945 started early. Warsaw was captured in January. A breakthrough was made into Silesia, and Kustrin, only forty miles from Berlin, was reached. Zhukov planned to take Berlin, but Stalin

Nomen est omen

'Secret – international – terrorist, that is the organization, and the name is Tito.'

DIE MAUSEFALLE

THE MOUSETRAP

This folk-story image of an old woman with a capacious skirt and petticoat comes from the old-established Kladderadatsch, *founded in 1848, only seven years after* Punch. *The old woman's skirt has 'Protection of small nations' written on it, belied by Stalin's appearance with a knife. It was published in 1944.*

GERMAN AUTUMN

A fitting epilogue to T.T. Heine's distinguished career as a satirist records his response in 1944 to the certainty of the end of National Socialism; Death shakes the Nazi leaves from the autumn trees. Heine had fled from Germany in 1934, and by 1944 was in Stockholm. A founder member of the Simplicissimus *staff, his anti-British satire in the First World War had been sharp-edged, and all his work of a high graphic standard.*

cancelled the plan. There was the possibility of a German counter-attack and the Russian lines of communication were threatened both from Poznan and Breslau.

Further south, Budapest was taken in February. In April Slovakia was cleared and Vienna taken. The assault on Berlin was planned for the same month, and began on 16 April. Hitler's suicide on 30 April was the prelude to a piecemeal surrender of the German armies. The war in the east finished when Jodl signed the German surrender document in Zhukov's headquarters in Berlin on 8 May.

National government was re-established in Czechoslovakia by internal and external forces, Czechs, Slovaks, Russians and Americans; and the independence of Prague was assured by the Russian emigré army under Vlasov, which prevented German units reaching the city. This action did not prevent the Russian authorities treating Vlasov as a traitor who was condemned and hanged. The American army reached Pilsen, but did not go further in deference to the agreement between the Allies that Czechoslovakia was within the Russian sphere. A national government on the model of the former republic was at first formed, but this gave way to a Communist *coup d'état* in May, 1946. Trieste was the subject of a dispute. The city had been captured by Tito's troops. The British and American view was that it should be returned to Italy. Stalin agreed to forcing the Yugoslavs to

THE MAN IN POSSESSION

withdraw; this was done reluctantly, and was a factor in the break between Yugoslavia and Russia in 1948.

Occupation of Germany and Austria did not prove contentious. The two countries were divided into zones for military administration. Control of Berlin and Vienna was shared by four countries, Russia, America, Britain and

This is one of those summary cartoons which describe a historical moment in time. Russian advances are the main topics of Strube's cartoon, but the shadow of the Second Front is visible on the floor behind the German soldier.

(right) *This Krokodil cartoon by Efimov shows a defeated German soldier returning in tatters from the unconquered city of Lenin.*

France. Previously agreed boundaries were held, by which British and American troops withdrew, in some instances distances of 120 miles.

The end of the war produced the boundaries of Eastern Europe which are still in existence – Germany divided, the Czech lands and Slovakia reunited, other states at former boundaries, including Austria given independence when freed from military administration, the Baltic states returned to Russia. The aftermath of the havoc of the war, most especially in the loss of

BACK FROM LENINGRAD

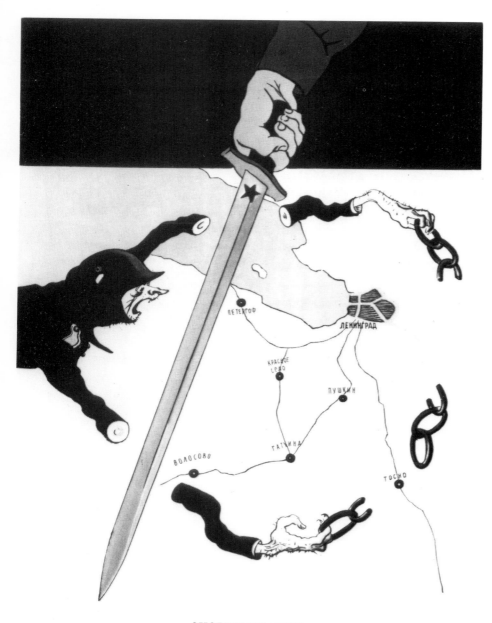

Raising the siege of
Leningrad is the subject of
this cartoon in 1944, with
the figure of a German
soldier and the sword of the
Red Army superimposed on
a map of Leningrad and its
surrounding towns as far as
Peterhof and Volosovo.
Kukryniksy have used the
pictorial device of a hand of
God to stand for the Red
Army, found in earlier
revolutionary images as the
hand of the worker.

SHORTENED ARMS

Hitler and Goebbels are seen swept away from the Polish city by a broom of swords in this 1945 cartoon by Kukryniksy.

KRAKOW NO LONGER OCCUPIED

life, was not, however, capable of recovery. The dead of Russia are variously calculated – at 11 million combatants and 7 million civilians; perhaps the figures should be much higher, another suggested total is 20 million. That would be two-fifths of the total death toll of the war, calculated with inevitable doubts, at 55 million.

Deaths of civilians from this time forward have a sinister and frightening possible meaning.

Fearful though deaths from high-explosive bombing or in a siege may be, systematic killing in the Nazi concentration camps had added a new terror of the inhumanity of man to man in history. There is a difficulty of scale in these deaths, which are listened to with incredulity. How is it possible to believe that in Auschwitz on a single day 24,000 men, women and children could have been done to death? The total death toll of perhaps ten million included

Krokodil *covers were an important feature of the magazine, as can be seen from this anthology: It appeared as a commemoration at the end of the war in 1945. Krokodil's readers included many who read copies pasted up as wall newspapers, which makes the similarities between a magazine cover and a poster more understandable.*

(**right**) *Hitler is seen by Semenov making a carousel go-round on which generals are seated or unseated over a map representing the east and western fronts of Germany. A newspaper extract accompanying the cartoon in a book of Semenov's work comments that to maintain his positions, Hitler resorted to changes in command 'almost every day'.*

those of the groups isolated by Nazi beliefs as being inferior to Aryans – Jews, Slavs and gypsy peoples. What measure of guilt should be attributed for these terrible actions to the propaganda which had poisoned German minds through Nazi publications from the first, for example Mjölnir's anti-Semitic drawings in *Die Angriff*, in which he pilloried a Jewish chief of police?

As for expression of horror at atrocities, this is a subject of more weight than the editorial cartoon can easily bear. It can be suggested that the editorial cartoon is a conversational medium, and its drama limited to the range of a good raconteur. For greater intensity of feeling, an artist of Goya's stature is needed.

THE STRICKEN CITY
'Your help is earnestly asked for the starving people of Warsaw.'

The text under this Punch *cartoon by Bernard Partridge then continues with details of where contributions should be sent for Lady Sinclair's fund. The figure of Famine, holding a flail, could have been drawn by Partridge in the First World War.* Punch *had a policy of occasionally providing free cartoon space for important purposes – another example was war savings.*

THE GENERALS' CAROUSEL

Chapter 8

FROM NORMANDY

The final act in the drama of the war in western Europe was slow to start. Stalin had been arguing for a Second Front from 1941, but the invasion was delayed for two years before final preparations were completed for Normandy in 1944. The first raid on the French Atlantic coast had been at Dieppe in 1942, and was a total failure. The Canadian troops sent into this operation were particularly unfortunate. For the purposes of German propaganda, Dieppe was a valuable asset, both in the press and on film, where the wreckage on the beaches gave eloquent witness to the repulse of the raid.

Preparations for the landings in France were successfully concealed. Two French invasions took place, one in southern France carried out by the Americans and French, and the combined attack on Normandy which Churchill, Roosevelt and Stalin had agreed would be the main invasion.

D-Day for the invasion was 6 June, 1944. 200,000 men were engaged in an operation which was backed by overwhelming air support. 156,000 men had landed by the evening of D-

DER WASSERSCHEUE KLEINE WINSTON —

**WATERSHY
LITTLE WINSTON**

The date of this cartoon from Neue Ordnung *is actually less than two months before the Normandy invasion.*

DE GAULLE'S TRAVELS
June 14, 1944: Mr Churchill, General Eisenhower, Marshal Smuts, etc.
visit Normandy while De Gaulle is barred.

Vicky here uses his command of English literature to portray De Gaulle as Gulliver among Lilliputians.

Day. Cherbourg was taken by American troops on 1 July, and Caen, which according to the original plan was intended to be captured on D-Day itself, fell to the British on 9 July. The invaders were warmly welcomed by the French, thousands of whom had been reading clandestine newspapers, two of which had taken for their motto a sentence by Marshal Foch, generalissimo of the First World War, 'No one is defeated except when he accepts defeat' *(On n'est vaincu que quand on accepte de l'être)*.

The invasion created a mood of despondency in the German High Command. The commanding general in Normandy, Rundstedt, was convinced that the war was lost. He was dismissed. Kluge replaced him, but Hitler wrongly believed him to have attempted to negotiate in August. He was recalled and committed suicide. Rommel also chose suicide on being confronted with evidence of his being implicated in an attempt on Hitler's life.

The attempt to assassinate Hitler was made on 20 July and miscarried. The man mainly responsible, Colonel von Stauffenberg, was shot, and the affair was minimized by Goebbels as the work of a small clique of disloyal officers. Goebbels had some respect for Stauffenberg: 'That Stauffenberg, it must be admitted, there's

**'He's from Ottawa, Sir!
Regular wiz at
unravelling red tape.'**

This is a cartoon for Maple
Leaf *by a popular
Canadian cartoonist with
the Canadian forces, Les
Callan. 'Monty' and
'Johnny' are his constant
characters; Montgomery's
companion is Private J.
Canuck, the latter standing
for the ordinary Canadian,
sometimes in the margin, at
others in the cartoons
themselves. The joke is
against the bureaucracy of
Canada's capital city,
Ottawa.*

a fellow for you! One might almost feel sorry for his fate. What coldbloodedness, what intelligence, what an iron will!' But this private opinion was not what he said in the broadcast about a 'horrible crime' which could have let loose 'a disaster…by the hand of a common criminal who, by order of an ambitious and unscrupulous little clique of adventurers and gamblers, had raised his hand to put an end to the life which is the dearest on earth to all of us.' For the Allied side, the assassination attempt was welcome evidence of opposition to the régime, and recreated debate about differences between the German people and the Nazi party.

Hitler was partly disabled, but his domination of the country's policies remained undiminished. One side-effect of the assassination attempt was increased power for Goebbels, who was given a new degree of responsibility for the total war effort. His measures included reducing the number of performances in the arts, reduced publishing output, a cut in the number of educational institutions and increased office hours in business and public administration. A member of his staff until the spring of 1945 commented on Goebbels' total war mobilization: 'How far did it succeed? Very far! It sounds hardly credible, but Goebbels' propaganda did keep the munition workers in the factories. In spite of the immense difficulties brought about by the air attacks, the intensity of the work still increased.'

The military history of the war in western Europe has been enlivened by different accounts

'Stoopid Frenchie'
(Maufais vranzais)

This drawing by Jean Sennep is on the theme of forced labour in Germany; the onlooker wearing a beret is an invented character called Count Adhemar, who is pilloried as a collaborator, as is his wife, Countess Hermengarde.

SCHALBURG'S DAY

The cartoonist G. Østerberg presented a copy of the book in which this drawing was printed to the Imperial War Museum. It is annotated as follows: 'A Danish officer named Schalburg gathered a corps largely comprising criminals. The corps was ordered by the Germans to perform acts of wanton destruction as reprisal to sabotage.'

(**right**) This cartoon was published in an anthology of Belgian clandestine drawings. The New York publication was called Belgian Humor under the German Heel.

of policies and plans of the different commanders, especially Eisenhower, Patton and Montgomery. Such conflicts were unknown to the public at the time, and were certainly not visible in cartoons. Evidence of Anglo-American differences were limited to the benign humour of Private Breger, or friendly jibes by Giles or Langdon. A main difference of view about strategy between Eisenhower and Montgomery was that, while the former planned a broad attack, Montgomery favoured a single thrust. By the middle of August there were more than two million Allied troops in France. A breakthrough with troops parachuted to Arnhem to outflank the Siegfried line failed. At the end of November the German line was firm, but the Allies had recaptured France.

'An automobile carrying two high-ranking German officers stopped on a road near Fornebu to inquire of a woman the way to the airport. "May I reply in English?" she asked. The Germans hesitated, growled among themselves for a moment but finally agreed. They turned to the woman for her answer. "I don't know", she said sweetly.'

The cartoon is attributed to Johan Bull, and was published in a Norwegian book in New York.

OUR POTATOES
'What are potatoes, father?'
'Look it up in the dictionary, son.'

PROPAGANDA

Pétain himself is seen writing propagandist graffiti. This acid comment about Pétain's Vichy rule was published after the liberation of France by Jean Sennep in an account of the war years, a book of drawings entitled In Honour and Dignity: Memoirs of Vichy. *Sennep lived across the river from Vichy; to which he daily crossed the bridge. His drawings were a way of expressing feelings which could not be shown; as the introduction to his book puts it, the period was especially painful since the army had represented an ideal of honour for him; and 'he understood that he had been betrayed'.*

The independence of France, however, was also due to the French themselves, whose resistance forces had made the capture of most of Brittany by Patton a formality. In Paris the Parisians regained their city; during August first the metro workers, then the police, went on strike; the resistance was called out. Hitler gave orders that Paris should be destroyed, but the German governor, von Choltitz, refused to obey him. On the entry of a French army division under Leclerc, he surrendered the capital to De Gaulle. The presidency of the Fourth Republic was calmly claimed by De Gaulle, who asserted that it had never died. The French nation rallied to him and the Communists gave him their support. There was a phase of civil disorder, in which 10,000 French collaborators with the Germans were executed. However, by the end of the year, De Gaulle had appointed prefects throughout France and the country was independent once more.

The re-establishment of the press, it was decided, would be based on clandestine publications or those which had been suppressed during the German occupation. The difficult ethical problem for journalists of whether to continue to write and work under German censorship had been solved in different ways. Against some of those who had continued to work, particularly proprietors and editors, action was taken in the courts. There were papers which had accepted that their role was to publish material provided by the German authorities; others had arranged to fall in with

Den kolde Skulder

THE COLD SHOULDER

Clandestine cartooning, such as this example by Osterberg, was dangerous during the German occupation of Denmark. Original drawings were difficult to hide, and many were destroyed for fear of discovery. A few were photographed and the film sent to London where they became propaganda material printed by the Ministry of Information; they were returned by being dropped from the air by the RAF.

'This damn tree leaks.'

This classic cartoon by Mauldin comes from the battlefield areas of northern France, depicted with equal exasperation by Bruce Bairnsfather in the First World War. Mauldin liked Bairnsfather's work, especially his sardonic character of Old Bill, with whom his own characters would have felt at home.

V DAY

This celebration of the day on which Germany surrendered is by Albert Dubout. He was a cartoonist who liked a little imaginative fantasy, which shows in a book of drawings of trains, and in his many book illustrations. The V symbol had been one of the successes of Allied propaganda in the war, from the chalked Vs that appeared on walls to the use of the morse code rhythm as a signal.

a system proposed by the Vichy authorities to follow a government line, which they had some freedom in interpreting. The line was made to bend. Then there were the papers which were suppressed, in the case of those with cartoons, *Le Canard Enchaîné* (suppressed in May 1940), and *Le Rire* among them. *Le Figaro* had been one of the papers whose offices were moved out of Paris to Lyon, but this did not prevent its suspension in November, 1942. The left-wing press was destroyed in the occupation years, but a clandestine press sprang up, including some papers with impressive print runs. A Catholic paper, with which Protestants co-operated, was *Le Courier Francais de Témoignage Chretien*, known to its later readers as *TC*. This monthly achieved a print run of 200,000 in 1944, and more for the liberation of Paris. The communist paper *Combat*, for 15 November, 1942, had a print run of 300,000, while *Défense de la France* in 1943 and 1944 had print runs of between 150,000 and 200,000. As the motto of *Combat* from Clemenceau put it, 'The last word in war as in peace is to those

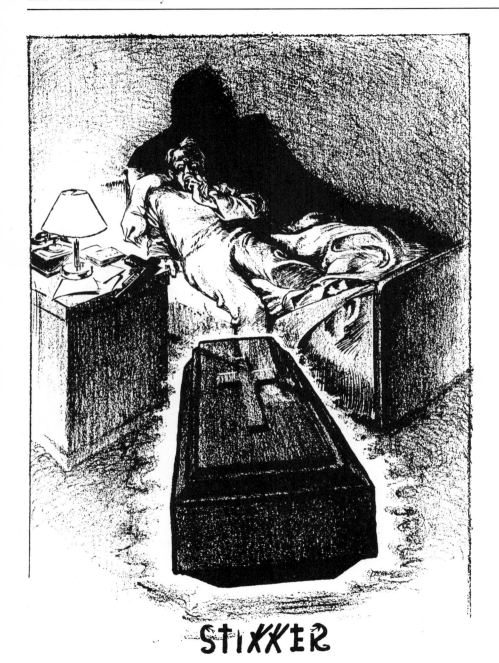

STIXXER

'Informer.'

This image was a cartoon with a grim purpose. It was posted in an ordinary envelope as a warning to informers to the German authorities. Österberg, the artist, took refuge in Sweden in 1944, where he continued propaganda work, including a poster of German military boots stamping on his native Denmark.

who never give up' *(Dans la guerre comme dans la paix le dernier mot est à ceux qui ne se rendent jamais).*

The ethical problem for writers during the German occupation was not shared by cartoonists, whose commentaries on events would have been prohibited if candid. There were only limited opportunities in the clandestine press, although there were cartoons in a *Combat Illustré*. Some bitter commentaries were published after the liberation, perhaps the most telling by Sennep, in his scenes of Vichy where some people have heads composed of the Fascist emblem, the axes as ears. The liberation of France also brought back to the country some cartoonists who had been with the Free French, such as Jean Oberlé.

In the middle of December, 1944, Hitler threw the dice for a last time. The German army attacked in the Ardennes. It became known as the Battle of the Bulge, the name for the narrow front of German penetration towards the Meuse. But by the end of the month Patton had recaptured Bastogne, while in the north a counter-offensive was effective with the help of air support against the German tank forces. Montgomery had been in command of the American troops in the north and created ill-will by claiming personal credit for the victory. Another inept piece of international relations was due to Eisenhower who ordered the abandonment of Strasbourg. De Gaulle countermanded the order, and Strasbourg was held.

The crossing of the Rhine, a naturally

'Don't come worrying us about this war when we're so busy on plans for the next.'

Osbert Lancaster satirizes relations between Hitler and his generals, making a point of the previous military history of Prussia, with books on the table giving the dates of wars, and pictures of war leaders, as well as a bust of the Kaiser. Cartoonists could only guess about degrees of responsibility for military plans. Hitler blaming others for failure was a common theme; his promotions to the rank of Field-Marshal was another source of jokes.

" Don't come worrying us about this war when we're so busy on plans for the next."

LAST FEARFUL HOURS

This allegory by Carey Orr mixes modern and medieval figures. Death receives the keys of Hitler's cell from Time; the setting is a murderers' row, and the bunch of keys has a swastika. It is perhaps doubtful if readers of the Chicago Daily Tribune *noticed that one of the cells is marked with the flag of Italy; in July, 1944, an ally of America against Germany; especially as the banner headlines in the issue concerned were 'Invade another Jap Isle' and 'US Troops battle into Pisa under heavy Nazi fire'.*

attractive landmark for cartoonists, was slowly effected by Montgomery by 23 March, 1945, but swiftly by the Americans over a bridge which had not been blown up at Remagen by 7 March. Eisenhower did not continue to Berlin, but advanced slowly, wrongly believing that there was danger of a Bavarian stronghold in which German resistance might be concentrated. There was also the political consideration that Berlin had been agreed as being in the Russian war zone, so its capture was left to Zhukov.

Montgomery advanced with British and Canadian troops to the north. Hamburg was captured on 3 May; then the Baltic coast was reached, Denmark thus being freed to re-establish its independence. The German northern forces surrendered on 4 May to Montgomery, while Jodl surrendered to Eisenhower on 7 May, and to Zhukov in Berlin on 8 May. The European war was over.

Suicide removed from the world stage several of the most prominent German leaders, including Hitler and Goebbels. Some others had longer to live, and a reckoning to make at the trials of war criminals at Nuremberg. Cartoonists there saw and portrayed men of evil. It is a moment of history which is well documented. Low was one of the cartoonists present and produced both cartoons and drawings of the prisoners. He commented on the appearances of the accused. He saw them as:

Very ordinary-looking in fact. If you saw them sitting opposite you in the train you would think all was normal. Also they were much too small. As we know, Nazi leaders used to attach great importance to their personal 'presentation', and under their rule the camera had evidently become the most efficient liar yet evolved.

This Kukryniksy cartoon is a variation of the Old Testament theme of the writing on the wall at Belshazzar's feast. The artist took a fierce dislike to Göring, 'the sleek, straight hair streaked back on the balding head, the womanish face, blotted and heavy-jowled, with patches of pink on the cheeks, the thin frog-like mouth orphaned of its lower lip and the little tin shifty eyes . . . his once powerful body had slackened and the cheeks sagged.' And as for Hess: 'A scrawny neck ended up in a sallow waxy face with black woolly eye-sockets and protruding nose.'

THE LAST FIGURE

Where is the great Göring, the jingle of whose medals used to keep the world awake of nights? . . . Well, Göring turns out to be about 5ft. 8in., still fat despite weight lost in prison; jolly, you would say, until you noticed the cruel mouth, vital, with periods of rumination when the countenance is sicklied over with desperate worry.

Göring stands out by a mile as the boss in this company. He is a restless prisoner, leaning this way and that, flapping his pudgy little hands about, patting his hair, stroking his mouth, massaging his cheeks, resting his chin sideways on the ledge of the dock. Göring is not permitted to make speeches, but he managed to get a good deal across with facial action. Nods, shakes, and eye-play suggestive of innocent l'il Hermann wrongfully accused.

In 1946 the war was over, and the immediacy of emotion about the progress of the war, so deeply felt at the time, had evaporated. A new pattern of post-war problems in international affairs was beginning to be seen, for which the war would only be background material. Interpretations of the campaigns on land, sea and in the air were formulated, and battles needed to be given official names by historians. At the time of an event, no one saw the whole picture, and sometimes even looking at the same picture, different people saw different scenes. Here is one of the fascinations of cartoon reading: what you see is not the whole truth, but it is what thousands or perhaps several million newspaper readers saw at a moment in history.

Chapter 9
TOWARDS NAGASAKI

By the summer of 1943 the Japanese drive south had been stopped, notably by the American capture of Guadalcanal. From this time the Japanese were on the defensive; an important personal loss was the death of Yamamoto, the ablest strategist in the Japanese navy; his plane was ambushed over the Pacific in April. Newspapers lost their earlier optimism; for example the Osaka paper *Mainichi* commented on 1 June, 1943: 'The desperate struggle on Guadalcanal, the gallant death of Admiral Yamamoto, and the heroic stand of the 2,000

This appeared in the New Yorker, *drawn by Alan Dunn, credited with more than 1900 drawings in the journal between 1926 and his death in 1974. The supremacy of the news media, in this case the film newsreel, has come in for sharp comment over the last two centuries at least. An American anecdote is William Randolph Hearst's reply to his war artist, Frederic Remington, in Cuba in the 1890s, when Remington complained that there was no war to draw: 'You supply the drawings and I'll supply the war.'*

'Paramount News sends its respects, sir, and could we move a little closer to the atoll?'

This cartoon by Minhinnick appeared in the New Zealand Herald *in January, 1943; it personifies the United States as Uncle Sam, here a soldier pointing the gun marked 'USA war power' away from the Pacific to Malaya.*

'Raise your sights, Sam.'

soldiers at Attu have clearly shown us the grimness of the war.' Belief in the invincible spirit of Japan was nevertheless firmly held.

The strategy of this part of the Pacific war revolved round the question of where the Japanese defensive line was to be held. By September it was intended to hold a line from the west of New Guinea and the Caroline Islands to the Mariana Islands. Concern was particularly felt about a base which would put American bombers within range of Japan.

During 1943 sea battles and island invasions slowly brought the conflict closer to Japan. The progress of the war was still at this time imperfectly known to the Japanese public, since control of the press caused the delay or suppression of news. In 1943 about thirteen per cent of the newspaper items submitted to the various censorship agencies were banned and the death of Yamamoto was not reported for five weeks. The situation was quite different from the propaganda war in Europe, where constant monitoring of enemy broadcasts on both sides created a competition which seized on inaccuracies and misrepresentation. Commentators in Japan on the war were not reporters in the front line; official spokesmen, such as the chiefs of the army and naval press sections, wrote newspaper articles commenting on events. The duty of a war correspondent with the Japanese army was to write stories about individual units, not to describe or comment on the progress or conduct of the war. The scarcity of news in turn tended to limit the responses of

A little number entitled, 'Yes, we have no Marianas.'

This parody of the popular cockney song, 'Yes, we have no bananas' was published by Armstrong in the Melbourne Argus *in July, 1944. The loss of Saipan drove Prime Minister Tojo out of office. The stereotyping of the Emperor in traditional dress was common in enemy cartoons. Armstrong was a popular editorial cartoonist in Australia, and published several collections of his wartime output.*

cartoonists to generalized patriotic propaganda.

Japanese cartoonists had only one main cartoon periodical at this time, *Manga*, edited by Kondo Hideo. Cartoonists were grouped in patriotic organizations, one of which was the sponsor of *Manga* and the other a more extreme group called *Manga Totsugekitai*. An example of a young cartoonist at the time is Oghara Kenji, who was precociously gifted. He joined the *Manga Totsugekitai* at eighteen, and then in 1942 went to serve in the Army in Burma and China. The job of an army cartoonist was partly to draw material which might help to demoralize the enemy; another task was to be an instrument of propaganda in the country to which he was posted. This was particularly useful in countries where there was a considerable amount of illiteracy. For Indians, who included some of the most disaffected people from British territories, some stridently anti-British cartoon material was produced. A versatile cartoonist whose work as a propagandist was far from his reputation as a draughtsman of sensual women was Ono Saseo who served in Java.

In Japan the needs of a wartime economy exerted pressures as severe as in Britain or Germany. War production was assisted by the messages of the cartoon strip *Suishin Oyaji* (Mr Promotion), and the Japanese exponent of

'Make do and mend' was *Omoitsuki Fujin* (Innovative Housewife). As for recruiting, the Japanese navy commissioned the country's first full-length animated film from Seo Mituyo, of whom the hero was a version of the famous folk hero, Momotaro.

Direct psychological war between opposing armies was in the end a greater success for the Allied cause. At the beginning of the war the Japanese military code had been so strong that almost no prisoners were taken. The classic instance was the defence of Attu in the Aleutians, which inspired the use of a powerful metaphor in Japanese, *gyokusai*, the breaking of a jewel, to describe fighting to the death. In the latter two years of the war, the pattern was altered, and limited numbers of Japanese troops surrendered. Leaflets about humane treatment for prisoners had some effect, though no doubt the military facts of the war were more compelling reasons. Among the devices used by Allied propagandists was a newspaper *Rakkasan Nyusu* (Parachute News), which included a fake of the gag strip *Fuku-chan* (Little Fuku). The real author of the strip, Yokoyama Ryuichi, in fact served in Java as a propaganda cartoonist.

The war in Burma had not been particularly active in 1943, for two British initiatives had been unsuccessful. Even Orde Wingate, who had mobilized northern tribes to support his guerrilla activities, found himself in difficulties; his forces dispersed and made their way back to India. The situation changed in the spring of 1944 with both Japanese and British armies

'An elder brother's duty.'

This cartoon by Kato Etsuro is a Japanese example of problems faced by every country in maintaining production. Schoolboys, drafted to work in factories, are shielded by an older worker from 'Temptation', as it says on the bottle of beer. As in other countries, graphic arts were used to encourage industry; there was a special name for this, zosan manga (production comics).

A Japanese appeal for saving metal is unexpectedly answered in this cartoon by a horse.

taking the offensive. During May and June these operations culminated in crucial battles at Imphal and Kohima; in the latter city the Japanese advance was stopped on the site of a tennis court in the Commissioner's garden; it is now a military cemetery, in which the lines of the court have been preserved. The Japanese lifted the siege in July. They had started with 85,000 men, of whom 53,000 were lost, against British and Indian casualties of 16,700. In the north a Chindit operation against communication lines at Indaw was successful, although Wingate himself was killed in a plane crash; and Chinese troops under the command of the American general, Stilwell, captured Myitkyina.

The Burmese war was an important British success, and a correspondingly severe shock for Japan. When Rangoon was taken in May, 1945, just before the monsoon started, the whole of Burma was in British hands.

From the summer of 1944 the Americans made decisive advances. In June a landing was made at Saipan in the Mariana Islands. With this landing was connected the battle of the Philippine Seas, mainly an air victory for the American navy. In Japan the naval command kept quiet about this defeat. But the loss of Saipan was unavoidably public news, and a significant indication to the Japanese public that all was not well. The Prime Minister, Tojo, and his government resigned, and they were replaced by a more moderate administration.

In October a major battle in Leyte Gulf confirmed Japanese fears. Leyte was captured by the Americans at the end of 1944; the rest of the Philippine islands followed the next year. MacArthur had kept his promise to return to the Philippines, and waded ashore on several

'Mr Promotion.'

He is a cartoon strip character by Matsushita Ichio. The factory boss is seen in mourning for the death of Yamamoto (1); a messenger tells him that the workers are agitated (2), and he is asked to write slogans to restore morale (3 and 4); his slogans include 'Never forget the Admiral' and 'Increase production in the name of our hero' (5); and he promises to write more (6).

beaches to prove it. He was in a position to lead an army, perhaps of 5 million men, into battle against the Japanese on mainland China.

The war for the Pacific islands in 1945 was strongly contested. One of the landmarks was the battle for Iwo Jima, a small but important air base, in February. There was also the long-drawn-out battle for Okinawa; this lasted for three months. Both these battles brought the war closer to Japan's mainland, and made the possibility of invasion a real threat for the first time.

From the Allied side, victory in the Pacific at last seemed realizable. The intricate jigsaw of strategy and tactics, by land, by sea and in the air, was at last making a recognizable picture. It had been the Americans and the New Zealanders whose operations succeeded in isolating Rabaul,

**IN MEMORY OF A GREAT DEMOCRAT AND FREEDOM
FIGHTER – FRANKLIN DELANO ROOSEVELT**

This marking of Roosevelt's death which appeared in Op
Hollands Erf, *a Dutch paper, is an example of the obituary
cartoon, which* Punch *claimed to have invented for the
death of the Duke of Wellington. It was a genre which had
some notable images in the First World War, more especially
in* Simplicissimus.

leaving 100,000 Japanese troops unable to
become re-engaged in the war. It had been the
Australians and the Americans who subdued
New Guinea. The war at sea had been successfully waged both by the USN Fleet commanders,
and also by the submariners whose damage to
Japanese merchant shipping had an important
impact on life in Japan. These heroes were quite
unsung, as the US Navy kept a rigid censorship
on submarine warfare.

MacArthur believed that the worst American
strategic decision of the Pacific war was the
separation of his military command from the
Navy command of Nimitz; they followed different policies, MacArthur hopping from island to
island, building an air base on each: Nimitz, on
the other hand, pursuing a more orthodox
military approach, attacking a stronghold in
force, as at Guadalcanal. In the end, however,
the combination of their strategies proved
conclusive.

There was some difference in the sustained
morale of the armies of the two sides. The
Americans could take comfort in their knowledge of immense resources of industry and
manpower at home. For Japanese servicemen,
victory was attainable through the power of the
spirit. This was the basis of a successful appeal
for pilots to carry out suicide missions against
American ships. They were nicknamed *kamikaze*,
after the divine wind which had saved Japan
from invasion by the Mongols in the thirteenth
century. Purification of the spirit was a strong
force in Japanese thought, with three main
strands – removing foreign influences from
Japanese life, living austerely, and fighting, that
is being prepared to die for the Emperor,
embodiment of the spirit of Japan.

These flying figures of Churchill and Roosevelt appeared in January, 1942. The animal hindquarters and tail are derogatory, the badger standing for cunning. Roosevelt's clothes are made of dollars, while Churchill's signifies death.

馬脚·狸尾
近藤日出造

HORSE'S LEGS, BADGER'S TAIL

The principle of purification finds expression in some cartoons. One example is a cartoon by Sugiura Yukio which appeared in *Manga*. A girl is seen combing out 'Anglo-Americanism' from her hair; among the words which have fallen in the dandruff on the floor are 'extravagance, selfishness, hedonism, liberalism, materialism, money worship, individualism' as well as 'Anglo-American ideas'. The quality of purity is also associated with the sword, for which a bayonet is a wartime substitute. It follows that a bayoneted figure in a Japanese cartoon has not just a bodily significance, but a spiritual one too.

Japan had been within range of bombers from American aircraft carriers earlier in the war, but the raid which marked a change of policy to fire-bombing was on 10 March, 1945, when Tokyo suffered an air raid in which 83,000 people were killed. In the last six months of the war it became increasingly clear to Japan's leaders that they faced overwhelming difficulties; but the Imperial Cabinet was divided. Unconditional surrender was demanded by the Allies, as Churchill and Roosevelt confirmed in a proclamation sent from Potsdam where they met in July. The essential difficulty was that the proclamation did not clearly state that the position of the Emperor would be preserved. A side issue was that the news

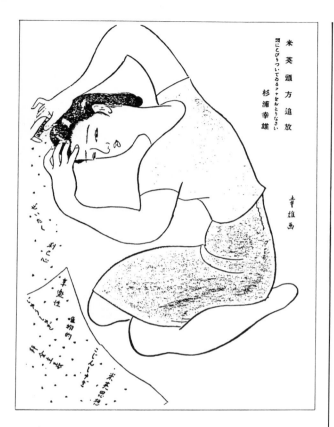

米英頭方追放

間にとびついてるラァ丸おとうならさい

杉浦幸雄

幸雄画

'Purging one's head of Anglo-Americanism.'

This patriotic image by Sughara Yukio appeared in Manga, *asserting the need to get rid of un-Japanese values including extravagance, liberalism and money worship. Outline drawing technique was standard for Japanese strip cartoons, though rarely so gracefully used as here.*

agency gave a misleading translation of the Japanese government's response: it was said in English that the proclamation had been disregarded, whereas the decision had been to consider it. Japan hoped for mediation by Russia.

The catastrophic end came in August. Truman, who had succeeded to the American presidency on Roosevelt's death, decided to use the atomic bomb, a weapon of an entirely different scale and character to anything in the previous history of warfare. The trial bomb exploded in the American desert had an explosive force equal to 15,000 tons of TNT. The first use of this type of weapon was on 6 August, 1945. The single bomb that was dropped on Hiroshima burned out more than four square miles (eleven square kilometres) of the city and killed perhaps 80,000 people, besides injuring more than 70,000 others; the second bomb dropped on Nagasaki killed between 35,000 and 40,000 people and injured as many more. Following the dropping of these two atomic bombs, Japan surrendered. The cabinet had been deadlocked on the issue, as the service ministers wished to hold out for better terms; the Emperor himself made the decision. Surrender was announced by Hirohito to his people, and was greeted with stunned bewilderment, accompanied by resignation. Militarists attempted at the last minute to destroy the recording of the Emperor's speech, but this was foiled. A formal surrender ceremony was held on 2 September, 1945, on the battleship USS *Missouri*. MacArthur was designated to head the administration of occupied Japan, a priority of which was to rewrite the constitution.

The full effects of the atomic bombs were not

The apparition of a Japanese woman with many arms to accomplish many jobs is by Ono Saseo. The cheerful energy of this image contrasts with his flapper girls of the 1930s, or the more sensuous westernized types he drew in the post-war period. The figure is less strange to eastern than western eyes since the Buddha and other devotional images can have many arms.

known at the time, but have now been systematically studied for more than forty years. An atomic bomb survivor is a *hibakusha*, and the message of a *hibakusha* is 'Peace from Nagasaki. May the second atom bomb be the last.' The psychological and emotional pain of the tragedy has been the unenviable subject of a number of works of art, in paintings and drawings as well as film. But one of the moving and effective means of creating understanding of the events and what led up to them is in *Barefoot Gen (Hadshi no Gen)*, a narrative in comic book form by Nakazawa Keiji, himself a boy of six in Nagasaki at the time of the bombing. His father, brother and sister were killed. Nakasawa's book began as a serial in a boys' weekly in 1973; it

fiercely describes both the scenes and emotions of people involved, specifically attacking militarism and war. Three live-action films, an animated feature film, and an opera have been made from the story.

No event had more potential significance for the future of the world than the development of the atomic bomb, and this was recognized universally. No editorial cartoonist could fail to respond to the occasion of their import. Rube Goldberg's later appraisal has been described. Norman Lindsay in the *Sydney Bulletin* resorted to personification; in his cartoon Nemesis says to Science: 'Little Man, what now? Take your choice! The end of war or the end of everybody and everything.' *Punch* had a cartoon entitled

LIFE OR DEATH

THE ATOM

LOW

'Baby play with nice ball.'

Low's cartoon appeared in the Evening Standard, *his response to the new fact of atomic power used for destruction in war. It answers his own criteria for a good cartoon, which included: 'Are the details nicely composed so that the eye slides easily to the full meaning? Has the drawing the appropriate blend of fantasy and realism to insinuate the satire? . . . Does the performance fit the intention – not too laboured to defeat the spontaneity; not so facile as to be insignificant?'*

'For Good or Evil'; it was drawn by Shepard and featured an angel and a devil fighting for possession of the sun, named as 'Atomic Energy'. Low produced a notably judicious response in a cartoon which pointed to the gap between the emotional and intellectual stages of development in mankind. On a wider front, it is worth reflecting that the existence of nuclear energy presented to cartoonists in an extreme form the problems under discussion at Low's lunch party described at the beginning of this book. What means are appropriate to symbolize such awe inspiring forces?

The problem is one with which we have become familiar through war cartooning, a difficulty of how to indicate scale in events. A space on a sheet of newsprint, or a page in a magazine, is finite, and cannot be extended or condensed like a book. A battle or an event in a war will be commemorated by a single cartoon, whether the numbers are relatively small like the 5000 men killed on either side at the capture of the Philippine Islands by the Japanese, or immense like the number of Russian prisoners taken by the Germans in their 1941 campaigning — 300,000 prisoners at Minsk, 200,000 prisoners at Vitebsk, and 520,000 prisoners at Kiev. The problem is compounded by that fact that an optimum number of figures to be used in an argumentative cartoon is not more than three, and many of the best cartoons are limited to two. In the case of Low's Hiroshima cartoon, his trick is to use everyday figures — the man in the white coat and the baby. They stand for intellectual power, the embodiment of Science, and emotional response, the embodiment of Growth and the Future; these personifications are implied, not explicit like Lindsay's Nemesis and Science. Paradoxically, the everyday figures are more compelling because they make an analogy; by playing down the scale of the problem of atomic power, Low's cartoon forces us to imagine its consequences.

In the years following the war a reassessment of Japanese customs and institutions was made inevitable by the American occupation. One new enthusiasm was for narrative stories taking the form of comics on the American model. A god of this novel world was Tezuka Osamu, a gifted film animator as well as a master draughtsman with a flair for judging what would catch the public imagination. His style as a film maker was originally based on Walt Disney, but he became an eclectic, and his large studio was responsible for work in many different styles. Tezuka wrote in his autobiography that after the war he had felt that existing comics were drawn 'as if seated in an audience viewing a stage, where the actors emerge from the wings and interact. This made

This is a page in a post-war comic book history of the aftermath of the bomb dropped on Nagasaki. The artist was Nakazawa, himself a survivor. The book was called Barefoot Gen *in the English version published in California (which has been translated and whose images are reversed to read in the western style).*

AMONG THOSE ABSENT

Illingworth's main cartoon in Punch *for the victory parade in London in 1946 pointed to two crucial facts about the end of the war. Illingworth became the outstanding editorial cartoonist of the* Daily Mail. *His technique included scraperboard to give sharp outlines and contrasts of black and white not obtainable in the quieter drawing he uses here.*

it impossible to create dramatic or psychological effects, so I began to use cinematic techniques... French and German movies I had seen as a schoolboy became my model. I experimented with close-ups and different angles, and instead of using only one frame for an action scene or the climax (as was customary), I made a point of depicting a movement or facial expression with many frames, even many pages.' This meld of Japanese and Western ideas and techniques has become common. There has grown up a massive comics industry which makes commentators today speak of a 'visual generation' in Japan.

This outcome can only be seen with satisfaction against the background of Japanese cartooning during the war, with its inadequate news content and absence of commentary except in the most propagandist tone. The variety of uses for comics in the 1980s makes a sharp contrast with the exclusive use of war cartoons as a tool of politics. As a Japanese writer put it, 'The flood of crude officially sanctioned "information" during the war years turned Japan into an intellectual insane asylum run by the demented.' The independent editorial cartoon also now has a status which was lost during the war.

Chapter 10

CARTOONISTS AND THE WAR

A partial history of the war can be made up, as we have seen, from editorial cartoons. This cartoon war does not match up either to the experience of participants or to the informed knowledge of later historians. Editorial cartoonists on newspapers are reacting to public news, supplied to them by others. Journalists are in a more favourable position, for they can often judge the merits of facts which they find for themselves. The cartoonist may in good faith inadvertantly omit facts or interpret them wrongly. If our view is widened to other sorts of cartooning, such as strip cartoons or jokes, the anticipated reactions of an audience may determine what feelings or general ideas they express. The outstanding advantage of cartoons is that they may stay in the mind long after chronicles of events or statistics have faded; a cartoon is often what makes someone say, 'Now I remember'.

All cartoons have value as historical evidence since they are documents in their own right; but like other documents they require careful interpretation. War cartoons need handling with kid gloves since it is especially likely that the cartoonist is not speaking for himself but for his paper, his class, his party, his group, or his nation. And, as in the Second World War cartoonists were very seldom women, wide swathes of feelings and views remain unexpressed.

What is shown by cartoons may also be limited in scope by technical matters. The ferocious schedule of a daily newspaper cartoonist is well known, but the time-lag of drawings for strip cartoons is less common knowledge. Martin Sheridan writing in 1942 described American practice: 'All comic strips which appear daily are drawn on a three-week schedule – that is, they must be completed at least three weeks ahead of publication. Sunday pages enjoy a two-month deadline. This lengthy deadline is set to allow time for the making of matrices and distribution of the strips in this form to newspapers all over the world.' Know this, and Terry's slow reaction to the Pacific War becomes more understandable. The most famous example of a time-lag dates from the nineteenth century, when *Punch* cartoons were drawn well in advance. In London it was thought sure that General Gordon, besieged in Khartoum, would be saved by the relieving military expedition. Tenniel drew his cartoon to show the happy outcome, which was decisively contradicted by history when the expedition arrived too late and found Gordon dead.

A further limitation of editorial cartoons is that, while any cartoonist has a rapport with his readers, that relationship may take different forms. Low was often at cross purposes with the readers of the *Evening Standard*, as his postbag proved. On the other hand. Strube was much closer in touch with his readers. It follows that for a historical understanding of a newspaper reader's reaction to world events (and the circulation figures for the *Daily Express* during the war were around two million) Strube is better value than Low. On the other hand, when Low had an inspiration, as in his memorable image 'The Two Churchills', he fuses a personal and popular view, while at the same time making an acute historical judgement. This judgement is a historical event; and the cartoon cannot be bettered as a way of remembering the British electorate's gratitude to Churchill in the war years, and its distrust of the Conservative party and its policies.

Other sorts of cartooning have different strengths and weaknesses as ways of understanding the past. Racism and imperialism are easy examples to take, both evident in Second World War cartoon jokes, or implicit in strip cartoons. A long-running series of a strip cartoon or a comic book story shows up shifts in

THE TWO CHURCHILLS

This is Low's excellent cartoon on Churchill's defeat at the post-war election.

*James Thurber's personal
drawing style delighted
New Yorker readers. He was
excellent at captions; once
he complained to the editor
about mere 'gag ideas'
which 'belong to the
laboured formula type'.
He believed: 'The really
great New Yorker cartoons
have had to do with people
sitting in chairs, lying on
the beach, or walking along
the street'.*

'He's been like this ever since Munich.'

public awareness of such issues. The historian may be especially interested in the implicit values in such cartoons, since these reflect general attitudes, as against more overt judgements made by an editorial cartoonist.

The aims of the cartoonists themselves have received rather little attention, compared with the labour lavished on even rather minor fine artists and their sources, their philosophies, and the development of their styles. Cartoonists who have also been book illustrators have perhaps been better served. A public attitude

has been summed up by an anecdote from a cartoonist. Having admitted to being a cartoonist, the next question was 'And what else do you do?'

The difficulty of comparison between painting and sculpture on the one hand and cartooning on the other is that their similiarities conceal important differences. Some cartoonists have distinctive styles of drawing, where the style is the man, say James Thurber or Saul Steinberg. Other cartoonists exploit their versatility and practice in many styles, as did Heine; mimicry

Ronald Searle produced an unexpected recruit for the Women's Auxiliary Air Force to appear in Lilliput. *This amusing work was not his best known wartime drawing; he was a prisoner of war in Japanese hands, and secretly made drawings which recorded his experiences; they were kept hidden rolled up inside bamboo poles. After the war he published forty of these drawings, which are graphic indictments of the treatment of prisoners and the conditions in the camps. He then resumed his career as a graphic wit, inventing a brilliant satire of a girls school, St Trinians; but his post-war work has a wider range than joking.*

can be a useful asset to a cartoonist in making a point. Other cartoonists again are able to move from cartooning to reportage or illustration, and may not be pleased to be classified narrowly as cartoonists. George Grosz or Ronald Searle are examples here of major twentieth century draughtsmen. The English language does their art an injustice in its failure to distinguish *humoristes* as the French do, or practitioners of *Karikatur* as in German.

The training of cartoonists has been very varied, from strict academic draughtsmanship to correspondence courses, these latter a feature of the American scene in the 1920s and 1930s, with tuition by some prominent cartoonists. The lucrative market for strip cartooning especially attracted ambitious youngsters. For example, Popeye in 1929 had syndication in 600 papers, and his creator Segar earned $2000 a week. The rewards were not so great in a smaller market like Britain; but in Russia cartoonists had an advantage of status as well as good salaries. A census of cartoonists' training would almost certainly give art school courses as the predominent background; but drama, literature, or other studies have also played a part, notably for editorial cartoonists. That uncertain quantity called general knowledge needs to be a constant resource for editorial cartoons, if their imagery is not to become stale or repetitive.

A further point about the status of cartooning is that the reproduction of a cartoon drawing, as

(**right**) *Fougasse used his figures wittily in cartoons like this. They also appeared in incidental drawings which helped to create the tone of his* Punch.

Isn't it wonderful to be . . .

getting . . .

out of . . .

the Services . . .

and . . .

back again . . .

to . . .

freedom! . . .

NORMAN MANSBRIDGE

This is an illustration to a parody of Alice in Wonderland.
*The drawing is by Norman Mansbridge, in an imitation of
Tenniel's original illustrations.* Adolf in Blunderland *was
the text of a radio 'cartoon', in which Alice is Adolf Hitler,
the March Hare is Mussolini, the Hatter is Neville
Chamberlain, and the Dormouse is the German people
(Doormat). The radio production was embellished by
selected music edited from 'Teutonic operas'.*

seen by newspaper or magazine readers has
been seen as the crucial event; the parallel is
with writing, where the publication of a story or
a book is crucial, and the fact of a manuscript is
less significant. Nor has there traditionally been
much of a market for original cartoon drawings.
Further, the degree of originality in cartoons is
not necessarily the same as for the work of a
painter. Take animated film, where the drawings
are the product of an extensive number of
studio staff, conforming to a studio style.
Consider the property rights in cartoon strips,
which belong to the publishing paper, and
which may be inherited by another draughtsman.

Looking back to the Second World War, the
editorial cartoonists held the most attention as
public personalities. Low was even enlisted in
an international attempt to push forward the
Second Front so much needed by Russia. He
received an open letter from his opposite
number in Moscow, Boris Efimov: 'I wish to tell
you, Mr Low, with what interest I and other
Soviet artists have been and are now following
your magnificent work, which has won for you
the well-deserved fame of the best cartoonist in
the world.' He replied in kind: 'I note in your
war cartoons, which I see frequently, your own
worthy response to the inspiration of the
present struggle.'

Low's international reputation depended on
syndication, an unexplored phenomenon in the
history of the war. Nor have the efforts of visual
propagandists been studied, apart from some
work on posters. A strong case could be made
for the more intensive study of cartoons, which
the recent establishment or development of
centres in Europe and America may promote.
For one thing, the availability of visual evidence

**'Tass window
number 747.'**

*This characteristic poster
format, with a rhyme on one
side and images on the other
was used from the 1917
revolution onwards. This
story, illustrated by
Kukryniksy, describes the
success of Russian partisans
in blowing up railway
tracks and German soldiers
with them. The heading is
'Fritz's Kaftan'.*

is about to change. At present looking at images in papers and magazines takes a great deal of time and physical effort. The technical possibility exists for images to be stored with new techniques, such as laser disks. The process can be seen at work already in the rather easier field of film study, where video recordings have helped to make possible closer and comparative studies, for historical as well as professional reasons. Will studying more cartoons create better historical understanding of, say, the Second World War? Surely so. The visual

1944

Semenov foresees the German leadership meeting catastrophe, in 1944, in a boat with Hitler at the helm and Goebbels as look-out. The many details include Pétain (with sticks on his back), Laval drinking, someone asleep with a sign saying 'I am only a passenger by accident', two men sitting on a log wondering how they can get dry; Göring hanging on to the side of the ship and a man with a suitcase who wonders where dry land will be.

evidence complements the incomplete written records.

Difficult questions about the past may be answered by such unexpected sources as jokes, not all of which are dead and buried. These queries may not be about rulers and politics, diplomacy and strategy, the old-established high ground of historical studies, but more everyday concerns. Cartoons can have a part in widening the range of our understanding of the past. 'Military history,' once wrote the historian Collingwood, 'is not a description of weary marches in heat or cold, or the thrills and chills of battle or the long agony of wounded men. It is a description of plans and counterplans: of thinking about strategy and thinking about tactics, and in the last resort of what the men in the ranks thought about the battle.' Contemporary cartoons are by definition not about plans and counterplans, since these were only known to leaders. It is only the culminating event, a battle won or a city surrendered that surfaces in the cartoon war. As for weary marches in heat and cold, that was precisely Mauldin's chosen type of theme in the *45th Division News*. The parallel case for closer attention being paid to visual evidence is oral history, for some time rather despised by academic historians with experience mainly of documents and with a preference for written evidence. But as increasing numbers of interviews have been undertaken, and with greater care than before, it has become plain that there are various sorts of information which can be got through interviews and in no other way. Part of the success of a boom in oral history has also been due to the increased technical efficiency of the equipment available.

A question that cannot be answered by looking at cartoons is what sort of role they played as agents in history. Occasionally there is evidence of the effectiveness of cartoons for some particular purpose, measured in the personal popularity of a cartoonist, some enthusiastic assessment, or a statistic of circulation figures. A systematic survey is definitely out of the question, for lack of appropriate material. Furthermore the effect of cartoons is impossible to separate from the effects of similar activities. Cartoons have to be left in the historical goulash called propaganda, adding a distinctive flavour to the dish. It can be safely asserted that cartoons added to the morale, the

PICA-DON

The title of this film about the dropping of the atomic bomb on Hiroshima combines light and explosion. It was made by Kinoshita Renzo, using drawings and photographs. The moment of this still is when children look up into a clear blue sky to see a single bomber flying overhead, one of twenty-four images needed per second in animated film. The transformations of human beings melted in intense fire is a searing memory of the film.

(left) *An Italian example of a strip cartoon used as propaganda. British rule in Corfu is described as leaving the islanders in 'squalid misery'; Mussolini is named as a* condottiero *(military leader in Renaissance times), and conquering Italians are welcomed as the German swastika flies over the Acropolis at Athens. Mussolini banned American strip cartoons in 1938, though the Italian Mickey Mouse* (Topolino) *escaped.*

NO PROMISED LAND

Pity is the key to Vicky's cartoon about the post-war plight of refugees. It appeared in the News Chronicle, *whose editor was not always prepared to accept Vicky's cartoons with grim themes. There was even a published anthology of those he had refused, entitled 'The Editor regrets'. This particular cartoon was republished in a pamphlet called 'Aftermath', where it was accompanied with quotations from the* Manchester Guardian, *about the refugees and their problems. Vicky's colleague James Cameron wrote of him: 'He was a man who carried always with him a mingled charge of delight and despair. He chose with us, his friends, to enchant us with the one and conceal from us the other.'*

will, spirit, or believed destinies of nations, but no one can say how much.

A few majestic claims have been made. Perhaps the most extraordinary was made in the First World War by Lord Northcliffe about propaganda, for which he had some responsibility. He asserted that propaganda had shortened the war by a year. A British Minister of Information in the Second World War told a different story of the low priority placed on propaganda. Duff Cooper wrote in his autobiography that he had difficulties with Churchill: 'when I appealed for support to the PM, I seldom got it. He was not interested in the subject. He knew that propaganda was not going to win the war.'

So far as war cartoons are part of the history of draughtsmanship, the cartoonists can only consider their war work as a short phase of their careers. Low, Efimov and Fitzpatrick were already well established before the war began, and they continued their practice as editorial cartoonists without a break. The war gave Mauldin his opportunity, and his success in the army enabled him to progress to becoming an editorial cartoonist after the war. On the art of a cartoonist like Giles, the war had little effect. He was on his way to creating the zany and memorable family with whom he has become inseparably linked. Perhaps the one effect of war on the cartoonists was a feeling that they were needed, giving their work a sense of purpose.

It could be argued, on the other hand, that cartoonists are needed just as urgently in peace, when they are able to take a part in debates on public issues; and satire is unusually good at deflating pompous claims or attacking bureau-

'I'd sooner they sent us a few pullovers instead of cartoonists.'

This concluding cartoon by Carl Giles was published in the Sunday Express *in November, 1944.*

editorial cartoons in context.

'The Press may be judged,' stated the report, 'first, as the chief agency for interesting the public on the main issues of the day. The importance of this function needs no emphasis.' The report went on to argue the needs of Britain: 'Democratic society, therefore, needs a clear and truthful account of events, of their background and their causes; a forum for discussion and informed criticism; and a means whereby individuals and groups can express a point of view or advocate a cause.'

Editorial cartoons in wartime are inevitably judged harshly by these criteria, since a clear and truthful account of events is impossible in a war, a time when the first casualty is truth. Nor is a forum for discussion wanted, especially not by governments. Defeatism, however, is wanted even less, so that one commodity in demand from any government is morale. Adversity is bad, but humour is a sovereign remedy. Cartoonists able to provide a laugh or two are popular both in war and peace; and there was laughter in every country, and in every theatre of the war. Sometimes cynical, from time to time bitter, often slapstick and occasionally witty, the cartoonists drew their times and the people in them. Usually with a gag, the visual quips lightened the burden of the war. The last laugh is certainly due to a cartoonist, in this instance a joke against himself. On 22 November, 1944, a cold and disgruntled soldier in a Giles cartoon for the *Daily Express* remarked 'I'd sooner they sent us a few pullovers instead of cartoonists.'

cracies and inefficiency. They are part of the press, with a job to do.

In 1947 a report was published as a result of a Royal Commission on the British press, about which anxiety had been felt for several reasons, one of them being that the power of a small number of owners had tended to increase. This concentration of power was naturally far short of the state control which we have observed in Germany or Russia during the war, but it seemed a threat. Two statements of principle about the press were included in the report which make useful touchstones for putting

MAIN REFERENCES
(Numbers refer to chapters)

M. Balfour. *Propaganda in War, 1939-1945*, 1979 (2)

C. Bellanger. *La Presse Clandestine*, 1961 (8)

E.K. Bramsted. *Goebbels and National Socialist Propaganda*, 1965 (3 & 8)

Al Capp. *Paintings* (exhibition catalogue, New York), 1975 (1)

R.G. Collingwood. *An Autobiography*, 1939 (10)

J.W. Dower. *War without Mercy*, 1986 (9)

Fougasse. *A School of Purposes*, 1946 (5)

Jon. *Two Types*, 1960 (4)

V. Lenin. *Collected Works*, VI, 1961 (2)

David Low. *Low's Autobiography*, 1976 (1, 8 & 10)

I. McLaine. *Ministry of Morale*, 1979 (1)

P.C. Marzio. *Rube Goldberg*, 1973 (4)

Bill Mauldin. *Mauldin's War*, 1951 (6)

S. Rogerson. *Propaganda in the Next War*, 1938 (1)

C. Rosner. *The Writing on the Wall*, 1943 (2)

F. Schodt. *Manga! Manga!* 1983 (9)

M. Sheridan. *Comics and their Creators*, 1942 (10)

B-A. Shillony. *Politics and Culture in Wartime Japan*, 1981 (9)

A.J.P. Taylor. *The Second World War: an Illustrated History*, 1976 (7)

C. Waugh. *The Comics*, 1947 (4)

STATISTICS

Many statistics in the war cannot be verified. No one will ever know exactly how many people died in the siege of Leningrad or the great fire-raid on Tokyo; in China the estimates of the war dead vary up to twenty-three million, while in Russia calculations are materially changed by the definition of Russian territory. As for battles, figures depend on what engagement within what period is defined as a battle.

Nonetheless, I have given estimated figures for deaths in the war, movements of populations, and circulation figures for newspapers. My aim has been to throw light on the scale of events, and knowledge of them through cartoons. A thoughtful discussion of the statistics of our violent times can be found in Gil Elliot, *Twentieth-Century Book of the Dead*, 1972.

CAPTIONS AND NAMES

Captions given with cartoons are normally those with which they originally appeared, but some captions are taken from later cartoon collections. Use for propaganda was one reason for altering captions.

Japanese names are given with the family name first. A few anglicized place names have been retained like Munich and Warsaw, but mainly they are transliterated; not always with complete confidence, as I have sometimes felt like a radio announcer in one of Lee's cartoons, 'Three other Russian places were reoccupied by our Allies, but the communiqué very kindly does not mention them.'

INDEX

Page numbers in *italics* refer to illustrations.